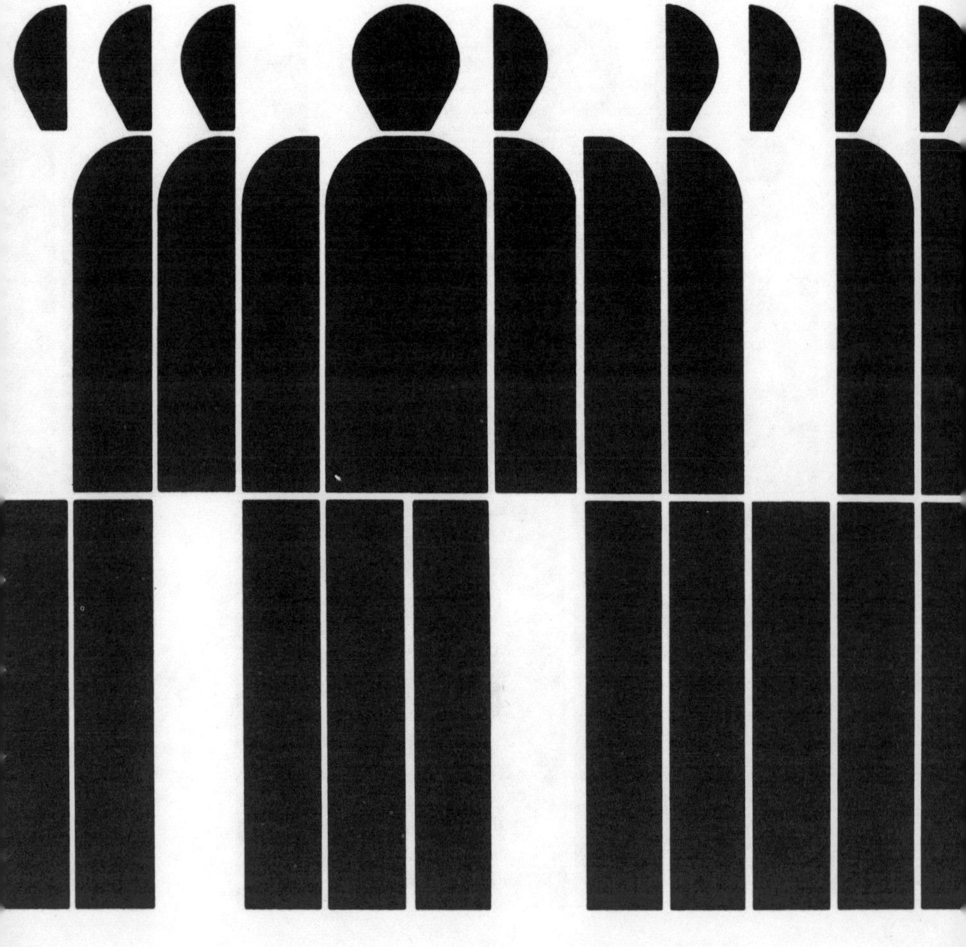

lee taylor, ph.d.

idea people

 Nelson-Hall, Chicago

003672

Library of Congress Cataloging in Publication Data

Taylor, Miller Lee, 1930-
    Idea people.

    Includes bibliographical references and index.
    1. College graduates—Employment—United States.
2. Education—Economic aspects—United States.
3. Intellectuals—United States. I. Title.
HD6278.U5T4   331.1'142   74-17805
ISBN 0-88229-149-1

Manufactured in the United States of America.

for
Jacquelin and Michelle

contents

This book is one product resulting from several exciting adventures the author has had over the past decade and a half living and working with the idea people. I have studied and researched many aspects of the work environments of idea people. I have shared problems and experienced joy with idea people. Most of all I remember challenges and look to the future with confidence and optimism largely because of my experiences with idea people. In this spirit I acknowledge the growth and reality of the pages which follow.

During the author's years in the late 1960s as Professor and Assistant Director of Research at Cornell University the design of this book was formulated. During that time I met with scholars, students, foundation officials, and major governmental agency directors. Also during that period I made extensive professional trips through Europe, Latin America, Canada and the United States. My life was touched and challenged by idea people the world over.

With these orienting experiences I have been called to be a part of the building of new academic programs. And most particularly related to this book, the author was appointed by two U.S. Secretaries of Labor, Hodges and Brennan, to play a role related to the National and Regional Manpower Advisory committees. Similarly Harold Dudley, the Commis-

acknowledgments

sioner of The Texas Employment Commission, appointed me to serve on the Policy Board of this agency. These national and state assignments have assisted in the refinement and release of material in this book.

In the final stages of the manuscript preparation, all or parts of the material was carefully read and critized by Jess Lord, Carl R. Golden, and Paul Steward. The author's wife Mrs. Jacquelin Taylor, gave critical and argumentative reading of the text. Dean Charles H. Green supported professionally our time for work on this book. Mrs. Diana Taylor typed the manuscript.

And as so often is the case, that which may be right, or meaningful, or useful in this book is the product of many. So much of what may be wrong must be the author's responsibility.

In January, 1974, political observer Joseph Kraft noted a significant development in the Nixon administration. The three most powerful presidential advisors—Henry Kissinger in the State Department, James Schlesinger at the Department of Defense, and George Schultz, Secretary of the Treasury—were not professional politicians. Kraft pointed out that they had one characteristic in common: before joining the Nixon administration they had been associated with high-powered academic institutions. This development did not receive any special attention. Only fourteen years earlier the Kennedy intellectuals were greeted with a great deal of fanfare, as was FDR's "brain trust" in 1933. What has happened during that relatively brief period is that idea people have moved to the center stage of American life, political and otherwise.

Just as the nature of an "idea" or a "concept" is difficult to understand, so are the individuals who generate them. But several of their characteristics should be evident. They are highly intelligent or highly trained, their work is primarily mental, and it is usually specialized and directed toward the world they live in. William Buckley's characterization of one of his old arch-enemies, John Kenneth Galbraith, serves as a good working definition of who is and who is not an idea

1

introduction

person. Galbraith, snipes Buckley, "always creates a sense of impatience, giving the impression that he is on very temporary leave from Mount Olympus, where he is conducting courses in the maintenance of divine standards."

Buckley's sardonic description is important for what it says and does not say. Buckley's evaluation aside, Galbraith is a highly trained specialist whose mental energy is devoted to improving his society, but one important distinction must be pointed out here. Idea people are not "intellectuals" as the term is popularly taken. Galbraith is not "on Mount Olympus" as a recluse; he is an activist, creating, disseminating, and applying his ideas. The same is true for other professions. An unknown poet might be an idea person; even if he does not actively propagate his ideas, he creates his artistic works to bring about greater awareness or to heighten the sensitivity of his readers to some aspect of the human condition or to stimulate others to act. Another poet, equally obscure, one who holds to the "art-for-art's-sake" view of literature, would not be classified as an idea person. This person views his art as food for thought, not for action. The same might hold true for two scientists. One might consider himself a "pure" scientist, who pursues and develops his abstract theories for their own sake, while another scientist may develop equally abstract ideas to improve society, even though he may not promote or apply them himself. It has been said that intellectuals live for ideas rather than off of them. For an idea person, the priorities are reversed.

It is the thesis of this book that in American society ideas are power, idea people are power people, idea people are both products of and producers of urbanized society, their roles are more normative than unique, and their social space is determined by both social organization and ideology. Accordingly, we conclude that the United States needs a manpower policy for idea people.

It is the purpose of this book, therefore, to study the origin and meaning of the vast social space provided idea people. This kind of study must proceed in terms of social organization in the context of urbanized society. It appears, therefore, that any social space society attributes to idea people is vastly legitimized by and largely in equilibrium with needs of the society. For example, many idea people either are scientists or are deeply influenced by traditions of science. Yet we hasten to point out that the founding of America and the establishment of its constitutional system essentially preceded science. The word "scientist" was not yet invented when America was discovered, but science and scientists have found, from the earliest days to the present, a propitious environment in America. By 1848 the associations of geologists and naturalists merged to found the American Association for the Advancement of Science. While this initial organizational move on the part of the scientists was essentially a merger of academic interests, it was followed quickly by powerful scientific in-puts into the society. Chemistry's molecular knowledge and insights, for example, led the way to fundamental changes and new dynamics in American industry.[1]

ideas as power

Science is neutral. It is not democratic. Neither is it responsible in the political sense of these terms.[2] Notions like democracy, communism, or totalitarianism are simply irrelevant to the basic nature of science. The discovered truths of science are not determined by political ideology or by what scientists themselves hope to find. In the most generic sense authority, whether it is political or professional, does not govern science. Accordingly, a discovery or insight by a naïve young scientist may exceed that of the most eminent older scientist.[3] Ideas are generically powerful by not ideologically powerful.

The neutral nature of scientific ideas enables them to be used for objective criticisms of political power.[4] In spite of this possibility, many idea people often hostilely reject political power. Others may join political establishments as experts and risk corruption of their knowledge base.[5] Idea power is often seen with clarity, even when accepted reluctantly. For example, the ideas of molecular chemists have vastly transformed American industry. Geological knowledge enabled the more systematic discovery of new mineral deposits and determined, for example, when the material could be most profitably used as fuel and as raw material for the manufacture of other products.[6]

In the administration of President Eisenhower, attempts were made to cut back expenditures for research and development. Nevertheless, during that administration Congress vastly multiplied appropriations for scientific research and development.[7] So alarmed at the power of ideas was Eisenhower that he admonished the nation when he was leaving office that it might "become the captive of a scientific-technological elite.[8]"

power people

The editors of *Fortune* have referred to researchers as the mightiest force in the U.S. economy. Scientific breakthroughs have given the U.S. population new antibiotics, missiles, polio vaccines, color television, power steering, wall-to-wall carpeting, jet transport planes, atomic weapons, and massive food production, to cite a few examples.[9] The powerful force of idea people is further expressed by the computations of Raymond Ewell of the National Science Foundation, who estimated that the U.S. has reaped 100 to 200 percent a year over the last twenty-five years on its scientific research investment. This astonishing estimate was based on the proportion of gross national product in 1953 which could be attributed to research achievements in the previous quarter of a century.[10]

The power of idea people in the form of a scientific revolution is overthrowing the nation's system of checks and balances.[11] The revolution being brought about by idea people is greatly more complex than the previous industrial revolution. In the case of the earlier one, governmental structures and other mechanisms to provide social order were designed to regulate and control economic entrepreneurs. Specialized scientists ultimately are not constrainable within political structures. Idea power is so great that there is considerable fear that constitutional processes may be undermined by cliques of scientists over whom the general public may have little or no control.[12] Certainly as the social sciences expand, unscientific value judgments in political decision making are placed in jeopardy. In the last twenty-five years, for example, court decisions have been increasingly influenced by social science data.[13]

The power of idea people comes from two directions. First, they are encouraged to leave their research laboratories and enter official governmental policy-making and staff positions. Secondly, administrators and political decision makers seek direction from evidence supplied by scientists. In neither case is the power ideological. In both cases the power is generated through expertise which is generic and neutral. In order to channel and optimize the effectiveness of idea power, social structures such as the Office of Science and Technology, the Council of Economic Advisors, and other similarly designed advisory bodies are being established. Their staffs are comprised of idea people who have direct access to decision making processes. Additionally, Presidents Roosevelt, Truman, Eisenhower, Kennedy, Johnson, Nixon, and Ford all have invited idea people advisors to their executive offices from basic research laboratories and academic institutions.[14] They are invited to put their ideas directly into action.

idea people and urbanized society

Idea people are both products and producers of urbanized society. In colonial days and in the early days of the Republic, inventors, scientists, and political leaders were often the same individuals. Men like Jefferson and Franklin exemplify that situation. Since then, there has tended to be a strong separation between political leaders and other idea persons.[15] During most of the nineteenth century, scientists were primarily concerned with what the general public viewed to be esoteric research into natural laws.[16] By the twentieth century, idea people had produced a body of knowledge so great that it has become a scientific revolution. Indeed there is evolving a new complex social and administrative order.[17] As early as the 1940s, Conant wrote that " . . . science had moved into industry and, belatedly, even in the United States industry had moved into science."[18] The major types of science research laboratories in private industries which illustrate these moves are those of General Electric Company, Bell Telephone Laboratories, and DuPont Company. The Department of Defense mobilizes large numbers of idea people to serve its needs, and other large government research agencies are developing. Idea people are modifying society, and society is demanding their service.

As the integration of idea people and the larger society become more recognized, and at times oppressive, policy statements have been made in attempts to clarify the situation. On the occasion of the one-hundredth anniversary of the National Academy of Sciences, John F. Kennedy said, "Scientists alone can establish the objectives of their research. But society, in extending support to science, must take account of its own needs."[19] In the 1960s when McGeorge Bundy was special assistant to the president he stressed the need for idea people. He observed that you don't solve nuclear weapons problems by separating them into component parts like science, defense, and politics. Solutions are achieved by bringing all the elements of a problem together.[20] It is hard to make more poignantly clear the fact that idea people are both the products and producers of urbanized society.

Policies concerning science and idea people have been proliferating in recent years. On the one hand, they aim to engender support for idea people. On the other hand, they attempt to protect the general citizenry from invasion of privacy. In both situations they represent the juxtaposition of society and idea people.[21]

This extensive integration of idea people and society is replete with both advantages and disadvantages. Ideally, the advantages are the providing of more support for idea people and more solutions for society's needs. The disadvantages involve the loss of ideals on the part of idea people as they become intensely associated with worldly power and the potential erosion, if not destruction, of freedom as the power of ideas supercedes governmental social control.[22] One may see an analogy in the relations of church and state which have ranged from integration to separation through the centuries.

the need for a manpower policy

America needs large numbers of professionals and executives to operate our urbanized and cybernating society. By their nature these idea people require the most extensive amount of training of any persons in the labor force in order to perform their roles for society. They constitute approximately one-quarter of the nation's labor force, and the results of their work disproportionately influence labor force patterns and behavior for all other workers. All of this is to make clear the critical importance of idea people in the nation's overall manpower. In spite of this important role, there is little or no manpower policy that is nationwide which relates directly to idea people.

In America the individual's opportunity to select his type and place of work has been traditionally regarded as a basic right. Only in times of critical national emergencies have people been restricted sharply in their employment and job mobility.

From a professional point of view, idea people are rugged individualists. The very nature of their work causes them to resist sharp policy definitions for their behavior. This is penetratingly clear when efforts are made to regulate, direct, or restrict occupational endeavors of physicians. They argue that they alone are competent to judge their own work. Most other major professional groups defend as their occupational prerogative the right and responsibility to define their own manpower situations.

Idea people receive most of their training in university environments. Universities, like the idea people they train, implicitly, if not explicitly, manifest a considerable amount of laissez faireism. They tend to be a curious mixture of the British tradition of educating gentlemen, the German tradition of producing knowledge for its own sake, and the American tradition of serving the needs of people who pay the bill for educational institutions. It is now probable that universities serve a fourth tradition, namely, the systematic training of idea people.[23] National ideology and professional associations both inhibit the development of a broad manpower policy for idea people.

The U.S. Department of Labor engages in a broad range of manpower activities. However, the Department of Labor is small, and its manpower programs are relatively new. The first specific manpower legislation was passed in 1962. Moreover, most of the manpower activities of the Department of Labor and of the fifty state-related agencies are oriented to individuals on the lower half of the occupational continuum, to unemployment situations, to urban poverty situations, and to specific training programs in skilled, semitechnical and some technical occupations. There are, in effect, no national manpower policies related to professionals, managers, executives, and many other occupational categories on the upper half of the occupational continuum.

There are studies of supply and demand for occupational workers at the idea end of the continuum. These are illustrated by: *College Educated Workers, 1968-1980* (Washington, D.C.: U.S. Department of Labor, Bureau of Labor Statistics, Bulletin 1676, 1970) and *Scientific Manpower 1960* (Washington, D.C.: National Science Foundation, 1961). There is a long and growing list of publications of these types. These reports contain estimates and projections of future occupational needs. They are, however, informational pieces which carry no authority and cannot direct specific action. Educators in universities may use these pieces of information as much to plan their strategies of competition as to curtail or accelerate their training in any specific areas.

The *Occupational Outlook Handbook* and the annual *Manpower Report of the President* are further examples of reasonably comprehensive documents which outline and develop profiles for occupations but with the greatest focus on the lower half of the continuum, although there is some attention to idea people. Like the publications that give projections and estimates, these documents are informational publications. They carry no authority for action. Accordingly, in the *Manpower Report of the President, 1970* there is proposed a new manpower-training act. Theoretically, it would create a comprehensive nationwide manpower service system. The new manpower-training act would have maximum state control and continue to be oriented primarily to the lower half of the occupational continuum.

idea people and educational policy

Idea people are individualistic and freedom oriented. Higher education, which provides the training environment for most idea people, is an utterly laissez-faire enterprise in the most rugged individualistic tradition. There is little agreement, and little drive to seek consensus, among educators concerning the most systematic ways to train high-talent manpower. Indeed, in some places there occasionally is virtual overt conflict among those who seek to maintain a learning environment free of any societal responsibility versus those who feel that the great state universities of the land ought to accept major responsibility for societal service. In other times and places, even when this type of conflict is not present, there is still little agreement concerning what is appropriate training for societal relevance.

While the above level of debate goes on, the enterprise of training high-talent manpower increases in magnitude and does become, if only by degree, more regulated and structured. In a recent study of state officials concerned with higher education, Eulau and colleagues submit that the entire process of education from elementary schools through graduate schools is now an integral part of the nation's political economy.[24] They point out that in 1966 the expenditures for higher education alone mounted to more than $15 billion. This may appear to be a large amount for training these individuals, most of whom will be idea people. It is, however, only 2 percent of the nation's gross national product.[25]

Theodore Schultz has developed an economic analysis of higher education and its relations to societal contributions. Schultz views education as a human investment. This is to say that it provides an improvement in the capacity of men to produce economic wealth. The health, technology, and financial capital of the nation are enhanced by the idea people training provided in the nation's universities. To the degree that higher education contributes through knowledge to increase economic output, it has advanced the economic growth of a society. Schultz argues that education is an investment in human capital just as a factory is an investment in physical plant capital.[26]

It was found by Eulau and associates that virtually all state officials whose work and/or committee responsibilities are related to universities agree that the state universities should be clearly linked to attracting industry to the states and to the providing of professional expertise for the state.[27] This is a view of opportunity, on the one hand, and need, on the other hand, for idea people. It is also a view which is implicit with conflict between societal expectations and the orientation of many idea people.

higher education

The greatest amount of financial support for higher education comes from the fifty states. Viewed from another perspective, the state colleges and universities enroll more than 70 percent of all the nation's students.[28] In recent decades, particularly in the 1960s, state legislators viewed higher education as a matter of considerable importance. Higher education expenditures were tripled during the 1960s, but much of the growth was caused by population expansion. Along with this expansion of financial support came a broad mandate for public service activities from colleges and universities which had problem-solving orientations designed to improve the welfare of the nation's people. These programs of state support for education and for public services have been highly productive within the states' rights format. Many legislative supporters of higher education and public service have been fiercely competitive in helping to build one state university system in competition with another state system, but there have been few instances of cooperative educational support and planning between and among states. Historically there have been a few notable exceptions where some states did not operate their own medical schools, schools of veterinary medicine, and schools of forestry. In these cases reciprocal arrangements were made to obtain training in nearby states.

To assist in the development and training of high-talent manpower in new areas of great need, the federal government has offered fellowships, assistantships, traineeships and research stipends of various types. In the absence of a definitive manpower policy for idea people, and in the absence of a definitive educational policy for idea people, the federal government has attempted through the Office of Education, the National Science Foundation and related agencies to stimulate training in areas of manpower shortage by providing funds for centers of excellence and funds for specific centers supporting basic and mission-oriented types of research. For many years some old-line agencies like the U.S. Department of Agriculture have supported specialized training. Specifically, for example, the Department of Agriculture uses Hatch Act funds to assist in training idea people through research projects. For briefer periods of time newer and smaller agencies like the U.S. Department of Labor and the U.S. Department of Housing and Urban Development have funded research centers and fellowships to open up new directions of inquiry and specialized training.

Finally it is important, and curious, to note that many legislators and executives who are well versed in the academic training process consider research of little importance in the training environment.[29] Indeed most American research is done in private industry. Nevertheless major amounts of important research, primarily basic, but sometimes also applied, are done by universities as a part of this training. There is competition among universities for research support. There is also a need for cooperative planning among universities to achieve maximum return on dollars invested in research training. One of the consequences of this lack of planning has been a regional "brain drain." Many idea people are trained in one part of the country, but ultimately are employed in other parts of the country. In other words, some regions train more scientists than they can use (see Figure

figure 1.1
geographical distribution of scientists by place of training and place of employment

states	number of research and development scientists	number of Nobel Prize winners in science	net gain or loss in physical science Ph.D.s
Alabama	865	—	gain
Alaska	161	—	gain
Arizona	650	—	gain
Arkansas	2,366	—	gain
California	13,688	21	gain
Colorado	1,415	—	gain
Connecticut	2,211	1	loss
Delaware	1,450	—	gain
District of Columbia	4,125	—	gain
Florida	1,470	—	gain
Georgia	762	—	gain
Hawaii	276	—	gain
Idaho	282	—	gain
Illinois	5,274	2	loss
Indiana	1,885	—	loss
Iowa	934	—	loss

idea people

12

figure 1.1 (continued)

states	number of research and development scientists	number of Nobel Prize winners in science	net gain or loss in physical science Ph.D.s
Kansas	578	—	loss
Kentucky	524	—	gain
Louisiana	844	—	gain
Maine	157	—	loss
Maryland	4,496	—	gain
Massachusetts	5,137	9	loss
Michigan	3,439	—	loss
Minnesota	1,734	—	loss
Mississippi	260	—	gain
Missouri	1,470	—	loss
Montana	279	—	gain
Nebraska	326	—	loss
Nevada	155	—	gain
New Hampshire	225	—	loss
New Jersey	7,030	3	gain
New Mexico	1,075	—	gain
New York	11,095	7	gain
North Carolina	1,345	—	gain
North Dakota	143	—	loss
Ohio	4,855	—	loss
Oklahoma	1,053	—	gain
Oregon	707	—	gain
Pennsylvania	6,317	—	gain
Rhode Island	370	—	loss
South Carolina	414	—	gain
South Dakota	125	—	loss
Tennessee	1,560	—	gain
Texas	3,368	—	gain
Utah	529	—	gain
Vermont	87	—	loss
Virginia	1,743	—	gain
Washington . .....✍	1,589	—	gain
West Virginia	683	—	gain
Wisconsin	1,652	—	loss
Wyoming	150	—	gain

Source: Ralph E. Lapp, "Where the Brains Are," *Fortune*, 73 (March, 1966).

1.1). The training of idea people has become such a large enterprise that its overall effectiveness can be enhanced by broad levels of regional and national planning.

The education of professionals and managers has been jealously guarded as the prerogative of professional educators. And as the body of knowledge in a specialty area is exceedingly esoteric it has been and continues to be very difficult for society to establish standards for education.[30]

Society, however, through agencies like the U.S. Department of Labor, the Department of Health, Education, and Welfare and the National Science Foundation develops projections and statements of need for idea people (see Table 1.1 and Figure 1.2). From time to time sharp differences are mani-

table 1.1

actual and projected demand for new elementary and secondary school teachers compared with number of college graduates, 1963 to 1978 (numbers in thousands)

year	total teachers employed	number required for growth and re- placement	new teachers required[1]	total number of college graduates[2]	new teachers required as percent of graduates
1963	1,806	209	157	444	35
1965	1,951	208	156	530	29
1967	2,097	222	166	591	28
1968	2,178	239	179	667	27
1969	2,225	209	157	755	21
1970	2,245	190	142-190	772	18-25
1973	2,286	189	142-189	859	17-22
1975	2,304	183	137-183	928	15-20
1978	2,334	187	140-187	1,029	14-18

Source: Based on data from the Department of Health, Education, and Welfare, Office of Education.

[1]Figures for 1963 to 1969 represent 75 percent of the total number required for growth and replacement, with a conservative allowance for the numbers of teachers who returned to the profession. Since the return flow of experienced teachers may possibly decline during the 1970s, the ranges shown indicate the numbers and percents of new teachers that would be required with a return flow ranging from 0 to 25 percent.

[2]Includes bachelor's and first professional degrees awarded.

figure 1.2

employment of scientists and engineers has grown steadily in research and development and other activities

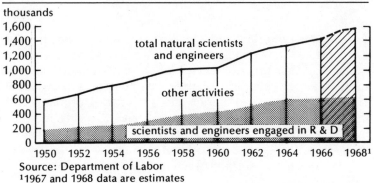

thousands

Source: Department of Labor
[1]1967 and 1968 data are estimates

fest between the projections and the training trends. There are both shortages and oversupplies, some of which are caused by the admissions standards set by professionals and training institutions. Articles like "35,000 Besiege Medical Schools; 13,000 Openings," in *The Chronicle of Higher Education* 6 (January 24, 1972), p. 1, illustrate the disparity between the control that idea people have over their own occupational space and societal projections of needs. This type of disparity is further illustrated when part of the pressure to pass the Emergency Employment Act of 1971 resulted from high rates of unemployment of scientists and engineers. On the other hand, there are examples of efforts by other professional associations to assess the need for their trainees and to increase or cut back the number of students admitted in the face of an undersupply or oversupply. This is clearly seen in the last few years in areas like the training of secondary school teachers where there is an oversupply. Many graduate schools are cutting back until the manpower needs and the training are more balanced.

All of these situations are characterized by the absence of educational policy related to the training of idea people.

I dea people in urbanized and post-industrial society have an important future and vast responsibility. As society enters the age of their pre-eminence a more precise, though necessarily flexible, definition of their characteristics is essential. They are characterized as individuals who work primarily with their minds—creating, disseminating and applying ideas. In the 1970s they are mostly male, but the number of females is increasing. The great occupational challenges in the foreseeable future are in areas characterized by mental exploration and exploitation.

professionals and managers

In terms of the labor force idea people constitute a large category. In the 1960 census they numbered nearly thirteen million persons, or 20 percent of the employed labor force, under the categories professionals and managers. In 1970, using the same census categories, idea people totaled over nineteen million and constituted 24 percent of the labor force. Projections to 1980 indicate some twenty-five million professionals and managers constituting 25 percent of the labor force.[1]

2

who idea people are

Census data constitute but one measure of the number and proportion of idea people in the society. If it were possible to measure idea and non-idea people more precisely, some students, some retired individuals, and some individuals listed under other occupational categories would be considered idea people. Similarly, individuals listed as professionals or managers would probably not be categorized as idea people if more precise measurements were available. Nevertheless, the census data constitute the best single statistical report of the number of idea people and the magnitude of their social space in society at any given time.

idea people and intellectuals

Aside from census data the common denominator of idea people is the mental quality of their work. Indeed, they have often been associated with intellectuals, notwithstanding the difficulties associated with defining that term. Like intellectuals, the general public simultaneously worships them as the hope for the future and fears them as a dangerous influence on the nation.[2] However, there is an important difference in the nature of their work. An intellectual, as we use the term, pursues ideas for their own sake, while an idea person pursues ideas with the intent of seeing them implemented, regardless of how esoteric they may be.

Although the tools for measuring the number of idea people are not exact, idea people are statistically visible and numerically of major importance in American society. They are not class conscious because they are too many in number and too widely spread to be well acquainted with each other. Even in professions in which there are thousands of practitioners, such as law, electrical engineering, elementary school teaching, or state public administration, only a few individuals personally know a great number of their peers. Still fewer are acquainted personally with creative people in subject areas outside their own occupational specialities.

By the nature of their work, idea people might be viewed,

who idea people are

by analogy, as the yeast of a society. Their pursuit of knowledge creation, dissemination and application is essentially individualistic. When their pursuit of ideas brings them into contact with their colleagues, their work tends to be characterized more by competition than by homogeneity. The main source of contact with their peers is provided by professional societies concerned about standards and ethics in their professions. While few forms of behavior are more difficult to judge for high ethical quality than the creation and application of ideas, the paramount concern for such a high standard of behavior continues unabated. Many checks, such as malpractice suits, are used by professionals themselves to insure high standards. Accordingly, where society is at all concerned about the orientation and purpose of idea people, it can most legitimately focus on their devotion to ideas for their own sake rather than for their relevance for or against any society.

In fact, however, there is an increasingly large proportion of idea people in America who seek active roles in which they can apply their knowledge to the problems of their society. A specific society and social climate can be a meaningful variable to the extent that it provides a conducive atmosphere for applying new ideas.

new ideas and the american spirit

Revolutionary America grew from new ideas, in particular the importance of the individual, spawned by the French Revolution. This concern for the individual coupled with an emphasis on growth and a future-directed orientation fostered by the Industrial Revolution have been imbibed in the American consciousness. This country has always been receptive to new ideas, especially those that can be applied to the betterment of the individual. Thus, it is to be expected that the work of idea people should receive substantial support from the general public.

It is also predictable that American thinkers would be individualistic and, while not necessarily liberal, opposed to conservative thought.[3] It is normative for idea people to be optimistic about the future, to question and often be critical of the present, and to hold past traditions generally in low esteem except to aid their perspective when making projections for the future. In essence this is to say that idea people by the nature of their work are less conservative or liberal and more explorers with a future orientation. In the day-to-day operation of a society, persons who are willing and who have a capacity to explore and anticipate future unknowns have a notably lesser capacity for custodial care of past traditions. Early in the twentieth century, psychologist James Lauba, studying the religious beliefs of members of the sociological, psychological and historical societies and of scientists listed in *American Men of Science*, found that a majority in each of these sample areas rejected beliefs in God or immortality.[4] In her 1953 study of scientists, Anne Roe similarly found that none of her subjects overtly indicated that religion was important to them.[5] They were not selected in terms of their religious background, but it was discovered that most of them came from traditional Protestant religious backgrounds.

Studies of voting behavior reflect similar nonconservative attitudes. In the 1930s other empirical studies found pro-New Deal attitudes among 84 percent of the professors of social science, 65 percent of professors of natural science, contrasted with 56 percent of the manual workers, 16 percent of lawyers, physicians, and dentists, and 13 percent of engineers.[6] In the mid-1950s, studies revealed that some two-thirds of university social scientists had voted for Stevenson when almost half of the manual workers and trade union members were voting for Eisenhower.[7] The voting behavior of journalists, another major category of idea people, tends to reflect a similar preference for liberal candidates, and artists of many kinds have generally worked and voted for liberal Democratic candidates.[8] Studies have shown that these creative people tend to manifest the most liberal voting orientations, while administrative managers tend to be less liberal in their voting orientations or at least more divided in their orientation.

who idea people are

When Lipset examined this overt manifestation of liberalism among specific segments of idea people, he attributed this to the American spirit of egalitarianism; he also contends that there is really no conservative tradition in America.[9] The traditions and social ideas of European societies were never in fact transferred to America, aristocracy and inherited social class position never having been substantive parts of American society. Consequently, idea people have never been considered members of a well-defined, elite group. From time to time American intellectuals have decried their lack of status as compared with their European counterparts. In fact, however, status in American society in general is achieved rather than ascribed, and intellectuals have not been discriminated against categorically.

If idea people constitute a new Brahmin element in American society, it is because they have achieved a high status by demonstrating the application of ideas to society. Their high status is awarded for what they can do rather than for who they are. Accordingly, creative idea people increasingly have been assuming powerful administrative and/or decision-making roles. On the other hand idea people who have traditionally been administrators or have been in positions of authority have moved into more creative, idea-producing roles. Although far from obliterated, the boundaries between the major categories of idea people—creative, professional, and administrative—increasingly are being blurred. The interchange of creative and administrative idea people is poignantly illustrated by the case of John Lindsay: when he became mayor of New York City, he appointed no fewer than seventeen college deans, professors, and lecturers to his staff in his first year in office.[10] This movement from the ivory towers to the marble halls represents a move to a different laboratory for observation rather than a basic shift in role perception. The case of a retired mayor of Boston entering the campus environment at MIT and stimulating a professor to write a book called *Urban Dynamics* and the case of a professor in Minnesota leaving the university campus upon election to the state legislature and subsequently writing a book on power structure illustrate the same phenomena—front-running idea people at the cutting edge of innovation, at new points of entry for mind stretching and new perceptions.[11]

Since the administration of President Kennedy, the opportunities for idea people to fill creative and administrative posts and apply their ideas to government and administrative posts have increased steadily. Many professionals believe this has precipitated a new and valid production of ideas that the most brilliant library or laboratory research never produces.[12]

The new action-orientated idea people are seldom guided by rules or constrained by operational manuals. They are often characterized by chance taking, impulse, ambition, discontent and public spirit.[13] Their careers are often volatile: an obscure individual may be elevated rapidly, and he may fall just as rapidly in the flurry of deposings, firings and other tactics that are used to eliminate individuals whose achievements are no longer recognized.

In 1967 Theodore White estimated that only a few thousand American college professors claimed membership in the action community.[14] A similarly small proportion of the managers and professionals claimed membership in the creative research and development idea community.[15] Yet this thrust toward new developments and relationships continues. New directions for mind-oriented activities among idea people are illustrated by the Rand Corporation. They take pride in the belief that Rand has bred a new generation of people with a new kind of problem-solving skill. It is the Rand position that "the way scholars think is as important as what they think about or what their thinking produces."[16]

This new focusing of the work of idea people is also illustrated by new ways of training. There are professors back on campus whose "sabbatic-type learning experiences" have included "instruction" as ambassadors (John Kenneth Galbraith in India and Edwin O. Reischauer in Japan), solicitors general, legal advisors to the State Department, special councils to the Department of Defense and so forth.[17]

who idea people are

New opportunities for idea-oriented work are being systematically expanded for women, particularly in scientific areas. Examples are illustrated by the 1964 Association of Women Students of the Massachusetts Institute of Technology Symposium,[18] which started locally and became national in its scope. Conferences of this type, and their subsequently published proceedings, furnish opportunities to acquaint women with careers in science and technology, to bring outstanding males into direct acquaintance with the concerns for women in these areas, and to encourage industry to use these people.

Especially in recent years professors have increasingly entered the engineering world as consultants, and practicing engineers have returned to the world of training on campus.[19] One example is at Southern Methodist University in Dallas. Faculty members from the Institute of Technology are encouraged to take industrial consultantships and engineers in industry are invited to serve as visiting professors. The intent is to provide faculty with practical professional situations and to bring more real-life relevance into the classroom. In another case engineers are participating in a "talk-back" television course, through which seven north Texas colleges and universities are making it possible to achieve advanced degrees while being fully employed in engineering firms. In this case most of the classes take place during working hours. Most participating engineers receive updated training and even advanced degrees without attending classes on campus.[20] Industry itself is enthusiastic about this kind of idea mix and accordingly provides time and money for its employees to participate.

In order to provide constructive interchange between top management personnel and creative people, an increasing number of universities offer full-time programs for executive development. These typically range from two to fourteen weeks.[21] Such notable schools as Stanford University, Massachusetts Institute of Technology and Harvard University provide major programs of this type. Approximately fifty additional schools offer similar programs. Another model for training idea-oriented executives is to provide "in-house" courses at major company centers. Two examples of this approach are General Electric's Management Institute at Ossining, New York and Motorola's Executive Institute at Oracle, Arizona.[22] In 1943 Harvard University inaugurated its advanced management program for senior executive officers. In 1961 it established a program for management development for younger executives. Each fourteen week course has approximately one hundred fifty students, with about one-third of them from outside the United States. They live and study together intensively for six days a week and have long periods of reading for homework each evening. These high-level, intensive courses are designed to prepare executives to be sharper idea people by asking more challenging questions. The course is directed toward *not* providing the selected executives with long cases of pat answers.

basic and applied orientations

The old division between basic and applied research is not relevant in discussions of idea people. The very notion of idea people includes both parts of this dichotomy. Some idea people devote themselves to "pure" research, which is often rather esoteric, while others with equal vigor concentrate on the application of basic ideas for general use in the contemporary society. The real world of inquiry for basic idea people is increasingly the same real world of action and professional people.

The problems and the intellectual challenges of mind exploration have required increasingly large laboratories, computer facilities for data analysis or libraries. The capacity to provide these resources typically far exceeds that of the individual. Accordingly, the government has provided these necessities and thereby the subject matter of investigation and environment supporting it have become highly integrated and, with increasing frequency, inseparable.

The nineteenth-century notion of the rugged individualist

intellectual who invented or explored on his own is inconsistent with the realities of contemporary society. Idea production is increasingly achieved by groups.

engineers

Idea people were accepted first in America; for instance, European universities did not even recognize engineering as a profession until long after American universities had customarily made such an acknowledgement.[23] Consequently, both mechanical devices such as computing machines and important abstract ideas such as cybernetics have been generated in America and have become an integral part of American society.

In 1970 engineers numbered 1,081,000.[24] Their numbers were exceeded only by elementary school teachers (1,260,000). Engineers far outnumbered nurses (688,000), clergymen (208,000), professors (550,000), lawyers (286,000), and physicians (266,000).

Over 70 percent of all engineers are employed in private industry. The next largest category, 10 percent, are federal employees, followed by 7 percent employed in educational and nonprofit institutions. The remaining proportion are employed in a variety of ways; some are self-employed.[25] Many engineers, 44 percent, have salaries that range from $10,000 to $14,999. Thirty percent have salaries ranging from $15,000 to $24,999, less than 3 percent earn over $25,000, and the remainder earn under $10,000. Electrical and mechanical engineering each employ approximately 20 percent. Almost 17 percent are in civil engineering, 11 percent in industrial engineering, 5.5 percent in aerospace engineering, 4.5 percent in chemical engineering, and another approximately 24 percent in a broad range of diverse types of engineering.

It is clear that this large category of professional engineering primarily represents idea people who apply their body of knowledge to societal needs. To a considerable extent, mathematicians, physicists and chemists provide the basic body of creative knowledge which engineers apply to societal problems. At the same time, however, the basic body of knowledge on which most engineering rests is rapidly growing and changing. More than once in the twentieth century engineers have been threatened by a so-called "half-life" body of knowledge. It is now increasingly apparent that, like managers, engineers must regularly and continually retrain themselves. Older engineers have experienced considerable unemployment. At times they have even threatened to unionize to protect their positions against younger men having a newer half-life knowledge. While it is expected that in the long run the demand for engineers to apply basic knowledge to societal needs will increase, it will also be incumbent upon them to be continually retrained and thereby be in a position to apply the latest and newest body of knowledge to our rapidly changing post-industrial society.

lawyers

For centuries the legal profession has been an idea profession. The number of people in the profession, including both lawyers and judges, has increased from 100,082 in 1950 to 200,012 in 1960 and to 286,900 in 1970.[26] Through the entire history of the nation lawyers and judges have been primarily appliers of a basic body of knowledge to societal needs. They have had a virtual monopoly on such services as drafting wills, probating estates, auto damage suits, criminal matters and taxes. Over half of the nation's lawyers work as private, fee-taking practitioners, most of them in individual firms. Their monetary remuneration from such small general practice averages about $13,000 a year. The elite of the legal profession are in a few large urban firms where partners have incomes that range typically from $30,000 to $75,000.[27]

The social involvement of lawyers is demonstrated most clearly by the large number who enter politics. Twenty-four of thirty-seven U. S. presidents have been lawyers, and 60 percent of congressional and state legislators have been lawyers. In addition to entering the political arena, men trained in law are often chosen to head major corporations, foundations and universities.

Like many other idea people, lawyers are guided in their practice by professional associations. The most important of these is the American Bar Association, which promotes a considerable amount of continual internal self-examination. Some of the key members of the profession consider the contemporary decline of ethical standards in the legal profession a major scandal. None less than the Chief Justice of the Supreme Court has complained that "law is failing to meet its responsibilities to keep the legal system functioning smoothly and to uphold responsible standards of ability and discipline among its members."[28] Lawyer-sociologist David Riesmen is quoted as observing that "probate is one of several areas of the law that is 'full of featherbedding. It is highway robbery'."[29] The American Bar Association has been an important forum for the dissemination of these new ideas.

Much to the impetus for change has come from the younger generation of lawyers. This new breed includes poverty lawyers, public interest lawyers, and movement lawyers.[30] Poverty lawyers are largely financed by government. They aid the poor and other victims of society who lack legal knowledge and as a result suffer discrimination. Consumer fraud, consumer credit, boycotts, and demonstrations are all major areas of concern for poverty lawyers.

Public interest lawyers are active in developing new tactics to pressure corporations into assuming responsibility for the safety, durability, and efficiency of their products. Ralph Nader is most exemplary of this new style of legal professional. The public interest lawyers have developed new ideas which are charging that public governmental agencies should establish regulations which consider not only economic questions but also social criteria ranging from fair employment to protection of the environment.

The third category of new lawyers is called the radical or movement group. These young lawyers represent political and cultural rebels including draft evaders, anti-Vietnam war groups, Black Panthers, Yippies, and others. These commune-type law firms are also committed to challenging inequities in the American Bar Association. In their work in criminal law they come into considerable conflict with old-line, established law firms. In some cases they are supported by foundations such as the Stern Family Fund, which supports the Stern Community Law Firm in Washington, D.C.[31] Some two thousand or more of the new generation of lawyers are reported to work in store front offices. In some major cities they are establishing counter bar associations which aim at both institutional and professional social reform.

It is difficult to imagine a more basic idea mix in reorienting the application of knowledge to societal needs than that being promulgated by the new lawyers.

scientists

Idea people in the sciences are clearly seen to include the most basic research scholars as well as action-oriented people involved in the development and application of ideas. The basic research scholars are found in Rand-type corporations, a few large industrial research laboratories, and in most major universities. Applied researchers are primarily found in major governmental agencies and in industries, although a smaller proportion are located in universities. Most scientists and engineers in government are employed either by the Department of Defense or the Department of Agriculture. The scientific personnel include persons in physical sciences, mathematics and statistics, biological sciences, social science, geography and cartography, psychology and operations research. Those in the engineering areas include general engineering, civil engineering, mechanical engineering, electrical engineering and a few others in a broad range of new types of engineering. The full range of health professionals are also found in government, mostly in the Veterans Administration.

There are sharp differences in the places where men and women are employed as idea people in the federal government.[32] The majority of women, over 80 percent, are in the health fields. By contrast only 2 percent are in engineering. Nearly half of the males, 47 percent, are in engineering while only 13 percent of the males are in the areas of health work. All three levels of idea people—creators, disseminators, and appliers—have exhibited among their numbers individuals who are both basic and applied professionals in their orientation.

idea people in power positions

Idea people are in the mainstream of power because they hold the key research and development positions which produce the new knowledge base on which society operates. Through their administrative and political positions, they implement creative research and development. Manpower projections indicate that employment requirements in the professional and technical occupations will continue to grow more rapidly than any other major occupational groups in the foreseeable future (see Figure 2.1).[33] In spite of this continued

figure 2.1
employment requirements will rise much faster in some professions than in others

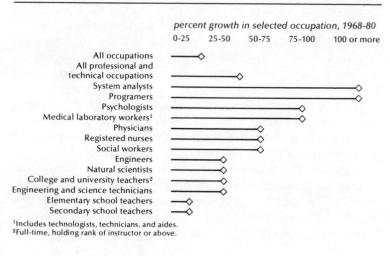

percent growth in selected occupation, 1968-80

| | 0-25 | 25-50 | 50-75 | 75-100 | 100 or more |

All occupations
All professional and technical occupations
System analysts
Programers
Psychologists
Medical laboratory workers[1]
Physicians
Registered nurses
Social workers
Engineers
Natural scientists
College and university teachers[2]
Engineering and science technicians
Elementary school teachers
Secondary school teachers

[1] Includes technologists, technicians, and aides.
[2] Full-time, holding rank of instructor or above.

rapid growth, it is expected that in the decade of the 1970s the supply of manpower in most of these areas will catch up with demand. The demand for systems analysts, programmers, psychologists, medical technologists, technicians and aides, physicians, nurses, and social workers will be greater than the average of all professional and technical occupations. In the professions, only the categories of elementary and secondary public school teachers are expected to grow less rapidly than all occupations in the nation.

Other projections indicate that the number of professional people in this country is expected to double in the next three or four decades but that the relative number of persons in sciences, engineering, the humanities and the arts is expected to remain relatively constant.[34] Put another way, idea people will continue to be a numerical minority in American society, even though they will exercise power far greater than their numbers.

The demand for technicians and paraprofessionals related to the major professions will increase dramatically. As the number of idea people grows, many old-line professionals will need increasing support personnel or back-up assistants.[35]

Although there will be little general growth in some professions like elementary school teaching, there may, however, continue to be significant opportunities for technical specialists like, for example, speech therapists.

In management the greatest opportunities will be in manufacturing where over six-hundred thousand administrators are employed. A close second is retail trade where another six-hundred thousand administrators work. Then there is a sharp drop to the banking industry where the administrators number just over two-hundred thousand and public official administrators who number just under two-hundred thousand. The other subcategories of management are smaller and range widely.[36] New job opportunities are related to these levels of current employment.

Another view of employment opportunities for idea people is found in the U.S. Department of Labor's *Occupational Out-*

look Handbook for 1972-73. Figure 2.2 illustrates the growth for professional and technical workers in the 1970s. Critical changes in idea production are being stimulated by specialists in marketing research, medicine, hospital administration, aerospace engineering, environmental science, conservation work, counseling and job placement, law, the performing arts, electronic computer work, social science occupations, urban planning work and journalism. All of these and other types of idea people are stimulating change and the development of new social structures in the power positions of society. Their actions are felt throughout the entire labor force, and the consequences of their work are seen in the changes they produce throughout the entire nation.

Generally speaking idea people's characteristics are upper middle class. One index of this position is indicated by a study of the 243,000 scientists listed in the *National Register of Scientific and Technical Personnel* in 1966.[37] Ninety-two percent of the scientists listed are male. Their median salary is $12,000, and the salary range is from $7,700 in the lowest decile to $19,700 in the highest decile. Thirty-seven percent of these idea people hold a Ph.D. degree, 30 percent a bachelor's

figure 2.2
during the 1970s, growth will vary widely among occupations

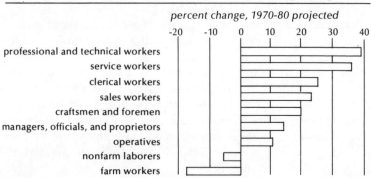

Source: *Occupational Outlook Handbook* (Washington D. C., U. S. Department of Labor, Bulletin 1700, 1972), p. 18.

degree, 27 percent a master's degree, 3 percent medical degrees, and 1 percent less than a bachelor's degree; 1 percent did not report degrees. Their median age was thirty-eight. Eighty-seven percent were in full-time civilian employment. Thirty-six percent worked at educational institutions, 34 percent in industry and business, and 10 percent in the federal government; the others had widely ranging places of employment. Thirty-three percent were engaged in research and development. Of these, 16 percent were in basic research and 13 percent were in applied research. Others were in research administration teaching, production and inspection and so forth.

A 1969 study reported in the *Monthly Labor Review* reveals the degree to which the scientific and professional personnel are in the mainstream of society from another perspective.[38] These data indicate that 71 percent of the scientific and professional personnel were employed by private industry, 14 percent by colleges and universities, 9 percent by the federal government, 3 percent by state governments, 2 percent by local governments, and 1 percent by nonprofit institutions. While idea producers may be disproportionally located in universities and nonprofit organizations such as Rand, the majority of professionals are in private industry where most of their work involves the application of ideas rather than the creation of them.

About one-fourth of the institutions of higher learning employ most of the research and development scientists. Most of these institutions are large universities with graduate programs in science, engineering and related fields.[39]

Studies of top leadership in the United States constitute another major index of the social status of idea people. Among the better known examples is Floyd Hunter's study of American leaders.[40] Although most of these leaders are in some way associated with general business and industry, it helps to see the idea-spread by noting the following affiliations: voluntary associations, thirty-nine (most of these are women who are voluntary civic leaders); college presidents and other college affiliations, thirty-three; banking organizations and firms, thirty-two; agriculture and agriculture journalism, twenty; journalism in the mass media, nineteen; prominent governmental leaders, seventeen; professionals including dentists and druggists, sixteen; religion and labor unions, six each.

The social activities of these individuals clearly illustrate why their influence is felt far beyond their own professional positions. These individuals function as conduits between their professions and the social agencies they work with. Many of these idea people periodically enter the idea environment at different places and bring new points of view. A small but significant number of university scientists and scholars from time to time enter the administrative ranks. Professionals, particularly lawyers, move between administrative and professional roles. There is also some role exchange between industrial managers and government administrators.

While women have made significant contributions to the advancement of ideas in society, their actual number is small. Aside from their general dominance in the voluntary civic organizations, school teaching, nursing, and library science, women are generally outnumbered in the other major idea areas. The tradition still continues that when a woman enters the professions she enters a man's world.[41] Or put another way, in the United States there are approximately a million and one-half persons working as professional scientists and engineers only about seventy thousand of whom are females.[42] But even the sex bias appears to be lessening as increasing numbers and a growing proportion of females enter idea-oriented occupations.

scientism—a forward looking ideology

Colonial America was founded in a spirit of new orientations and liberalisms, reflecting considerably on the importance of the individual as an outgrowth of the ideology of the French Revolution. The new American nation continued the ideology of a future orientation, a posture of growth and building, more than a traditional or ruralistic culture. In effect the American nation was born during the Industrial Revolution and has continued to be a dominant part of that forward-looking ideology. Therefore it should be anticipated and is normative that a maximum amount of social space is given by society to idea people. They are doing precisely that which is most widely expected in America. The American spirit has not been anti-conservative as much as it has been oriented toward exploring the future, the unknown.

It is the nature of creative people to explore new ideas. By definition creativity means developing new directions, scientific discoveries, and establishing new forms of social equity and environmental quality. It is therefore predictable that idea people will often vote for so-called liberal political candidates.[43] It is also predictable that idea people are not a bloc vote; they are by the nature of their occupational roles independent thinkers, and their pattern of future orientation and liberal political attitudes varies issue by issue and from time to time. Indeed most idea people work well within the traditional framework of society even when they are being critical of some of its institutions.[44]

post script—past idea people

Prior to the twentieth century, idea people were usually inventors rather than scientists. Moreover those who were scientists generally toiled alone or with a few assistants.[45] All of this changed in the twentieth century, when an individual scientist-engineer or an individual inventor needed a total environment in which to work and be stimulated. This new environment became so large, complex, and costly that individuals could no longer provide it. The telescope, computer, or cyclotron increasingly went beyond the means of individuals.[46] The independent idea people of the nineteenth century found their counterparts in the twentieth century increasingly beholden to government, business, universities, and foundations to provide the equipment and large environment necessary for the more complex areas of production.

In the nineteenth century both the scientist and, to a lesser extent, the inventor were considerably isolated from society. Until the middle of the twentieth century most college training provided an individual with knowledge that was adequate to sustain him through his lifetime. By mid century the knowledge base created by idea people had been amplified to such an extent that obsolescence became an increasing problem for the learner. Science and invention in the nineteenth century had been relatively isolated; it was an individual pursuit in society. By the middle of the twentieth century, technology had been expanded sufficiently on a scientific basis so that neither scientists nor inventors could continue to be isolated from the mainstream of society; individuals and their contributions became social institutions almost overnight. This is clearly illustrated by the application of electricity to individual machines and to industry. For some time scientists and inventors had been experimenting with electricity, but for society at large it had remained a mysterious force. By the end of the nineteenth century and the beginning of the twentieth, electricity became a widespread technology, first in factories and then in homes. All people—indeed society—acclimated to it. As a result of this type of mass production, dissemination, and application of ideas, factories became in effect a new type of environment by the end of the nineteenth century. As society attempted to integrate these new environments men like Frederick W. Taylor developed ideas and wrote books concerning principles of scientific management for relating people to machines.

Viewing it another way, Conant submits that in the nineteenth century popular credit went more to the inventor than to the scientists. This situation, he asserts, was true not only in the United States, but also in Great Britain. Possibly only in Germany were physical scientists being recognized for their own contributions.[47] In the nineteenth century scientists were esoteric individuals who primarily focused their attention on discovering so-called natural laws, while inventors took scientific discoveries and applied them to practical ends. "The attitude of James Clerk-Maxwell, the founder of the electro-magnetic theory of light, towards the inventor Alexander Graham Bell was one of patronizing condescension. (Clerk-Maxwell referred to Bell as 'a speaker, who to gain his private ends, has become an electrician.')"[48]

While scientists in the nineteenth century were generally looking down upon inventors, scientists were held in similarly low esteem by both inventors and the businessmen who backed their successful enterprises. By the turn of the century scientists were still getting only meager recognition. During World War I, for example, President Woodrow Wilson appointed Thomas Edison as chairman of a consulting board for the Navy. To this consulting board Edison appointed only one mathematician "in case we have to calculate something out." Similarly during the period of World War I, the American Chemical Society offered assistance to the Secretary of War. Upon investigation, the secretary returned to the society a statement of thanks, indicating that the War Department already had one chemist.[49] By the 1940s and the period of World War II, this nineteenth-century type of isolation for idea-oriented scientists ended. Science had moved massively into industry. There were great research laboratories functioning in organizations like the General Electric Company, the Bell Telephone Laboratory, and the DuPont Company. Similarly government was employing research scientists in large numbers.

Executive or management types, on the other hand, have been in the social mainstream since the founding of the nation. For the leaders of the new nation, ideas involved action, and it was a period when Protestant meant exactly what the word spelled. Harvard graduates had led the Boston Tea Party in 1773, and it was a new brain trust which invented the Constitution of the United States. This was a time when few men went to college, but among the fifty-five delegates to the

who idea people are

Constitutional Convention, thirty-one were college graduates. Six had been college professors or tutors, and three dozen had been lawyers.[50] These delegates were idea people who sought to develop a new form of government for a new nation.

America's idea people continued the tradition of innovation and protest during the period between the Civil War and World War I. Francis Russell in his book *The Confident Years* explains how America was catapulted from isolation and obscurity into world leadership by its idea people. It was a period when the billion dollar corporation was invented, when new industrialization spawned slums, and when mundane and grandiose technological inventions from the bicycle coaster brake to the Wright brothers' airplanes established a new content for American culture and consumer life. During that period was born both the bane and blessing of contemporary society—a complex and intensely urban society moved in mysterious ways by idea-oriented specialists for whom we do not yet have a comprehensive national manpower policy.

The origins of idea people are difficult to trace. By the nature of their work, they are mavericks, highly mobile and typically outstanding achievers at an early age.[1] It is important to know who becomes an idea person and why he does so. Answers to these questions will help to stimulate and direct an appropriate number of persons into specialized training and help to promote the development of appropriate training and planning policies for these individuals. The high career mobility of most idea people necessitates better planning to assure that a sufficient number of idea people will be where they are needed when they are needed. Any refined analysis of the origins of idea people must take these characteristics into consideration.

social class origins

Many idea people have had considerable upward social mobility. Mills reports that they are often farm boys who have made good in large cities and who now reside in suburbs, while many others have come from poor immigrant families.[2] This second kind of background is particularly characteristic of executives and administrators.

In spite of the foregoing information concerning upward mobility, most idea-oriented executives in the second part of

3

origins of idea people

the twentieth century were born with big advantages. Their fathers typically were at least in upper middle class occupations and with similar levels of income. They are disproportionately Protestant, white, and American born. Most have had disproportionate advantages for good education both at the precollege and college levels.[3]

In spite of the magnitude of privilege into which many people are born, the impression must not be given that they constitute a leisure class. They are a dynamic and productive people who think differently, do the unusual, work long hours, and generally manifest a strong sense of responsibility. Even though they occasionally may have a considerable amount of leisure, it is so interrelated with their research, business, administration or other work that it is difficult for them to differentiate between work and leisure. Even among the more wealthy a great amount of time is devoted to social service. After having achieved considerable economic security and recognition, many idea people devote much or most of their time to voluntary social services and/or to the amelioration of societal and governmental problems.

The opportunity for idea people to achieve great wealth— indeed to become millionaires—is considerable. Some do in fact amass remarkable economic fortunes. As a social class, however, idea people fall far short of great economic wealth either by inheritance or by achievement. They tend instead to be comfortably middle and upper middle class in their economic status. As a social class idea people are characterized more by their high educational achievement than by great wealth. Their way of life is dominated by mental activity. Most achieve high initial education, at the college level or above, and many continue their formal education and pursue learning virtually to the end of their lives.

Idea people possess the traditional advantage and status symbols of the middle and upper classes. Most of them live in the suburbs, have high-quality health care, are members of selective social clubs, and travel extensively, both for intellectual stimulation and leisure.[4] Often idea people participate extensively in cultural affairs—music, art, the theater and so forth. The character of their social life and status symbols reflects personal preference rather than conformity. In the main their social class characteristics are more "in" than "out." They are fast-moving people in a fast-moving period of history. Their style of life includes the "briefing," the "digest" and short memorandums. They are "talkers," "listeners," "readers," and "writers."[5]

There is one major exception to this pattern in the social origins of idea people. Union leaders often come from working-class backgrounds. Their homes were frequently poor, indeed often found in urban slums, and they often had little early opportunity for quality education. Accordingly, most early union leaders were not even college graduates.[6] While most other idea people whose origins were in the lower classes have experienced considerable upward social mobility, labor union leaders frequently are excluded socially from the middle classes. While many may ultimately enjoy considerable wealth and possess the major status symbols, they do not usually associate with the upper middle class. Labor leaders are in a peculiar position: They represent people in lower and middle social classes, but the majority of their professional work is with the upper classes who are their intellectual equals. This relatively small but significant category of idea persons in effect defies a convenient social class categorization.

While a majority of idea persons can be categorized into the middle and upper middle class, it must be clear that many are not only mavericks in terms of ideas, but also in terms of social class. For a great number of idea people the very notion of social class is objectionable, and their idiosyncratic behavior is a conscious rejection of class identification.

family origins

Among the most famous studies of origins of idea-oriented scientists are those by Roe.[7] By regional place of birth, Roe's sixty-three eminent scientists were distributed as follows: midwestern states, twenty-five; eastern states, twenty; western states, fourteen; and southern states, four. In her study of physical scientists, biologists, and social scientists, she found that all had been married at some time in their life. They usually married later than is customary in the U.S.; most of them had children. Divorce was fairly common, but varied considerably: 5 percent for the physical scientists, 15 percent for the biologists and 41 percent for the social scientists.[8] Thirty-four of Roe's eminent scientists had fathers in the professions, twenty had fathers in business, eight had fathers in farming, and two had fathers in skilled labor. Many of the scientists felt intense personal isolation in their youth. The extent to which these feelings persisted over long periods of time and are, therefore, different from those in other individuals in the population is unknown.[9]

It is reported in the Roe data that the IQ range of these scientists extended from 121 to 177. The median IQ was 166. At a comparable time Phi Beta Kappa members registered a median IQ of 137 while Ph.D.'s had a median IQ of 141.[10]

In a more detailed study of physical scientists Roe selected and studied twenty-two individuals. Eighteen of their fathers were professionals. Many of the mothers also came from families which included a number of professional men.[11]

The scientists generally expressed feelings of strong independence from their parents and, furthermore, a conspicious lack of guilt concerning their independence.[12]

A high degree of education, specifically college, was taken for granted by virtually all of them. Following the completion of their doctoral work, they generally experienced a steady professional development. The development of their intellect accelerated while the development of their social interest seemed to be passive. Accordingly, most were found to marry later in life than was generally true of the American population. Even after marriage a low degree of importance was placed on social occasions and social interaction with one possible exception being a strong concern for their children. The Roe studies indicate that her scientists were far more absorbed in their work, although it was frequently articulated as being fun, than in family and social relationships. Work was their way of life and it was engaged in so intensively that other considerations were of secondary importance.

Studies of social scientists indicate that they come from relatively high status family backgrounds. Lazarsfeld and Thielens, for example, found that 25 percent of their social scientist subjects had fathers in managerial occupations and 23 percent had fathers in other professional occupations. Another 15 percent came from small business-white collar backgrounds, 15 percent from manual labor backgrounds, 13 percent from farmer backgrounds, and 8 percent from teacher backgrounds. One percent did not indicate the occupation of the father. Even these data, which reflect the origin of professors at all universities in the United States, contain a considerable bias because many of the most distinguished idea professors are at the larger graduate universities where the socioeconomic backgrounds of parents are reported to be even higher. For example, at schools of nine thousand students or more, 62 percent came from managerial and professional families.[13]

Studies of senators indicate that at the turn of the century a significant proportion of their fathers, 35 percent, were proprietors and officials, 32 percent were farmers, and 24 percent were professionals. At that same time the general population distribution was: 22 percent, farmers; 7 percent, proprietors and officials; 6 percent, professionals.[14] There were some significant differences reported for the parental background of Republican and Democratic senators (see Table 3.1).

Matthews points out that probably less than 5 percent of the American people have an opportunity to enter the U.S. Senate. They come from a special class of people: they are predominately rural, Protestant, native born, upper middle class and college-educated lawyers.[15] Further it is found that the senators come from politically oriented families.

origins of idea people

table 3.1

occupations of fathers, by party and "class"

fathers' occupations (by "class")	Democrats (percent)	Republicans (percent)
professional	(28)	(19)
lawyers	16	7
M.D.	5	2
minister	1	6
professor	1	0
engineer	1	1
journalist	1	0
teacher	1	1
poet	0	1
government official	0	1
proprietor and official	(30)	(39)
manufacturing executive	0	3
publisher	0	6
merchant	14	17
banker	3	3
insurance—real estate agent	7	3
construction contractor	3	1
railroad official	1	2
other	1	2
farmers	(33)	(31)
low salaried workers	(3)	(0)
salesman	1	0
clerk	2	0
industrial wage earners	(5)	(7)
printer	0	2
carpenter	0	1
painter	0	2
barber	0	1
cigar maker	0	1
tailor	1	0
shipfitter	1	0

table 3.1 (continued)

fathers' occupation (by "class")	Democrats (percent)	Republicans (percent)
millwright	1	0
janitor	1	0
construction laborer	1	0
unknown	(0)	(3)
totals	100	100
	(92)	(88)

Source: Donald R. Matthew, *U.S. Senators and Their World* (Chapel Hill: University of North Carolina Press, 1960).

age

The relationship between age and creativity remains largely an enigma. In general it seems that creativity peaks in the late thirties or early forties. Furthermore, in the more abstract subject areas such as mathematics the peak ages of creativity are as early as the late twenties. In subject areas such as history the peak ages of creativity are as late as the middle or later forties.[16]

In the mid-1950s detailed studies were made to relate age to idea creativity.[17] Science and mathematics experts were asked to identify the most notable creative accomplishments. In areas like oil painting, education, philosophy, and literature, expert judgments were made by studying the created or written materials. For the several fields studied, the maximum average rate of highly superior productivity is listed below by ages:[18]

physical sciences, mathematics and inventions
chemistry, 26-30
mathematics, 30-34
physics, 30-34
electronics, 30-34
practical inventions, 30-34
surgical techniques, 30-39

biological sciences
botany, 30-34
classical descriptions of disease, 30-34
genetics, 30-39
entomology, 30-39
psychology, 35-39
bacteriology, 35-39

major administrators	U.S. Senators in 1925, 60-64
presidents of American colleges and universities, 50-54	men in charge of U.S. Army from 1925 to 1945, 60-64
Presidents of the U.S. prior to Truman, 55-59	Justices of the U.S. Supreme Court from 1900 to 1945, 70-74
U.S. Ambassadors to foreign countries from 1875 to 1900, 60-64	Speakers of the U.S. House of Representatives, from 1900 to 1940, 70-74
	Popes, 82-92

These data are not firm evidence that high idea productivity does not continue for some individuals into the older years; moreover, it is exceedingly difficult to obtain concensus concerning the criteria to be used in evaluation.

Lehman suggests some possible causes for the apparent early periods of creativity:[19]

1. Prior to age forty physical vigor begins to decline.

2. In middle ages and beyond, impairment of vision, hearing, and so on are frequent deterrents to high productivity.

3. Serious illnesses, often chronic, occur more frequently in the middle and the later years.

4. Glandular changes continue throughout life, and there may be changes in body chemistry which stimulate and deter high productivity.

5. In some cases marital problems and sexual maladjustment may reduce productivity.

6. Some older individuals may become increasingly indifferent toward creativity due to the demise of loved ones.

7. Older people, more than younger ones, may be preoccupied with the practical concerns of survival.

8. A result of success may mean promotion in administrative directions and leave less time for creativity.

9. Younger persons may be driven more for prestige and recognition.

10. Early fame and recognition may lead to complacency.

origins of idea people

11. Apathy may increase due to the deadening effects of nonrecognition.

12. Older people generally tend to be more inflexible than younger ones.

13. Older people experience a decrease in motivation and perhaps a weakening intellectual curiosity.

14. Younger individuals may tend to have better formal education and to be challenged by more stimulating problems and cultural environments.

15. In some cases psychoses may cloud an otherwise brilliant mind—a condition more associated with later years.

16. Finally, in some cases, an individual's creativity may be dissipated by alcohol or narcotics.

While the phenomena of age and creativity are far from understood, it is clear that in sensate urbanized societies, young adults often have the advantages that had traditionally rested with those in the upper years of life. As men seek to modify both their biology and society, it may well be that the relation of age to creativity will be subject to considerable manipulation.

religion

According to the overall evidence, most idea people have little direct association with organized churches. The existing evidence serves primarily to indicate the concern which idea people place on their work rather than on matters like religion. While intensively engaged in creative work, idea people give little attention to other activities including organized religion.

In Roe's study of scientists she reports that none of her subjects were selected because of their religious interest or affiliation.[20] Nevertheless, questions were asked concerning their religion. Most of the sixty-four scientists had come from Protestant parental background. Five came from Jewish homes, in one case the parents were reported to be strong "free thinkers," and none were from Catholic families. These scientists indicated that the intensity of religiosity in their homes varied greatly. Children, however, were sent to Sunday School.

In Roe's later study of physical scientists only a few were found to be churchgoers.[21] Furthermore, only two were specifically emotionally involved in an established church.

politics

The political concerns and political involvements of idea people are much more demonstrative and frequently more involved than their religious concerns. Organized religion is voluntary in America. Generally speaking, if a religious institution does not allow and/or condone intellectual inquiry, its members will either leave that institution for a more permissive one or leave organized religion completely.

Political organization, in the short run, appears more essential to the conduct of life in the urbanized society. Vast numbers of people are involved in the management of urbanized societies. A great proportion of these are themselves idea people. In addition to the idea people who are directly involved in the organization of society, society increasingly supports the research, development, and the dissemination of ideas. Both directly and indirectly virtually all idea people have played prominent and influential roles in politics.

Idea people and their work recognize no political limits. Researchers may desire to be "a bunch of guys having the greatest possible fun." They may interpret their work as ideas for ideas' sake. Society may "officially" attempt to provide for basic research, yet in America many idea people promote the usefulness of their ideas for society. And from time to time there may be considerable political pressure for idea people to work on specific problems and social projects like the National Science Foundation RANN (Research on National Needs) program. In juxtaposition, during the McCarthy era there was a considerable effort to control the freedom of idea people.

From the individual's point of view it appears that most idea people do not play active parts in political or civic organizations. However, most of them do vote and from time to time modestly align themselves with a political party.[22] In the 1960s some considerable investigation was made into the political orientation of selected categories of idea people like political scientists, psychologists and sociologists.[23]

A survey of members of the American Political Science Association in 1959 revealed that three out of four said they were Democrats. Indeed out of 213 respondents 137 were registered Democrats, 34 were registered Republicans and the remainder either preferred to be independent or had a preference for a major political party but were at the time not registered members. Only 4 were affiliated with minor parties—three Socialist and one Liberal.

Further analysis suggested that the political scientists had come disproportionately from families with a Democratic background. Only six of the political scientists who reported that they were Republican had changed from Democratic to Republican. It is further found that the Republicans generally teach in the smaller academic institutions.

In summarizing the origins of creative people one must return to our starting point; namely, they are mavericks and they are unique. Nevertheless, one may observe some very general characteristics. Typically they have not come from backgrounds of great wealth. Those who are not at mature ages were born predominately in the Midwest. They expressed considerable family isolation in their early years. They manifested precocious behavior early in life and achieved notable creative recognition between the ages of thirty and forty. Usually they come from Protestant religious backgrounds and in the fullness of their careers express little rigorous adherence to organized religions. Many idea people come from somewhat conservative political backgrounds, but tend to associate themselves with somewhat liberal political positions.

Practically all idea people in American society receive formal college training. Most obtain at least a baccalaureate degree. Many continue on to professional and/or graduate schools. In addition to this regular formal training, idea people often continue training throughout their careers by participating in seminars, short courses, professional meetings and so forth. Further, in addition to these school and school-related training programs, there are formal on-the-job training programs and informal job-related learning experiences. Very few idea people reach prominence with little or no formal academic training.

advanced education and the knowledge explosion

In the recent decades the college training of idea people has been generally satisfactory. One index of this is the report that 80 percent of the 8.7 million workers with three or more years of college education utilized their major subjects in their work.[1] Society has provided several incentives to encourage individuals to follow careers in areas in which there has been a need for more trained professionals. Since World War II, for example, the federal government has designed and funded numerous kinds of monetary grants, fellowships and

4

training idea people

traineeships to encourage advanced academic study. Furthermore, the federal government has increased its design and support of programs to provide funding to colleges and universities in order to develop teaching, laboratories, libraries, and other facilities. International competition in such areas as economics, military preparedness, food production, space exploration has contributed to the expansion of training programs. In the past, professionals received all of their training early in life—in their first twenty-five years—and then pursued their careers. Prior to the knowledge explosion of the second half of the twentieth century, this model was satisfactory. In the second half of the twentieth century, however, it has become increasingly apparent that the accelerated rate of knowledge accumulation necessitates more continual training throughout life rather than a block of training in the early years.[2] Society now needs more highly trained idea people and in juxtaposition the body of knowledge needs to be and is expanding at a rapid rate.

Accordingly in areas like the physical sciences and engineering, those trained in the 1950s at an undergraduate level are largely out of touch with nuclear physics and many other space sciences necessary to succeed in the 1970s. Similarly most of the computer technology has come into existence in the second half of the twentieth century. So rapid has been this change that an official of Westinghouse Corporation picturesquely describes the situation by suggesting that engineering graduates have a half-life of knowledge. About half of what they learn will be obsolete in a decade, and half of what they will need to know is not even available when they are initially in school.[3] This phenomenon is recognized throughout professional areas. Older men in the field become outdated quickly if they do not regularly participate in retraining.[4]

While the older idea people may come to have more experience in certain areas, the obsolescence of their knowledge erodes their effectiveness quickly unless they regularly participate in continuous training. This erosion of the knowledge base is experienced by idea people in administration as well as in the professions. Furthermore, traditional training programs, isolated in universities, are often marked by considerable measures of irrelevance in the real world as the dynamic urbanized society changes rapidly. Accordingly, the need to bring faculty and students closer to the world in which their specialties are practiced has become increasingly apparent. Increasingly many areas of study are started in the traditional, on-campus training environments but enriched by considerable off-campus field or laboratory experience in engineering firms, central slums, neighborhood health clinics and so on.

As idea people expand their domination of urbanized society, the many forms of continuing education that presently exist must be expanded into a major new model replacing the traditional form. Educational resources, teachers and facilities must be shifted to a pattern of continuous training. Some of the specific forms for continuing education might be: a program of national sabbatical leaves for six months to one year, training for one week in each month, training for one day in each week, training for one hour in each day and so forth. The range of combinations is considerable, and since no one form will be adequate for all idea people, several different forms of continuing education must be established for different areas for individuals at different stages in the life cycle.

In general these various programs for continuous training ought to be paid for by society and/or as a part of the regular work experience. At early ages in idea careers job training and "up-dated" training should be frequent. As people become older job training should be less frequent and general education should be increased. Indeed it should be anticipated that some individuals will become satiated with training at an earlier age than others. Presumably the number of people participating in continous education will decrease as individuals become older and opt not to continue the struggle for mind expansion.[5] Learning in the idea occupations is both stimulating and difficult. While it appears that over the last century the capacity for idea learning and idea work has increased for many people, there is reason to believe that some people will reach a saturation point.

Chamberlain submits that society can afford increased idea training. The expenditure will in effect be a form of self-liquidating investment.[6] Conversely the urbanized technological society is unable to afford inadequate training for idea people. College educated workers are expected to increase through 1980 and beyond.[7]

The number of professionally technically trained people during the 1970s will increase faster than any other major occupational category. Their rate of growth is expected to be approximately 40 percent due primarily to increasing needs of our complex society for specialized skills. The number of managers, officials and proprietors will increase by approximately 15 percent during the seventies. Approximately one-fourth of the expansion in the managerial category will be for growth while the remainder will be for replacement. About half of the average annual job openings through 1980 for professional and technical workers will be due to growth while the rest will be needed for replacements. The number of persons employed in professional and technical occupations from 1960 through 1970 and projected through 1980 are illustrated in Figure 4.1.

Although the professions will be the most rapidly expanding occupations in the 1970s, there will be considerable variation in supply and need in particular areas. For example, in the largest single profession, elementary school teaching, which employed 1,260,000 persons in 1970, mostly women, there will be an oversupply. Engineering, the largest profession for men, employing 1,081,000 persons in 1970, will experience some areas of overproduction. In the 1960s the federal government and other support sources stimulated the growth of both elementary school teaching and the engineering profession by providing student stipends and numerous grant programs to training institutions to expand their efforts in these areas. It appears that in the 1970s there will be little or no overproduction of idea people at the baccalaureate level,

idea people

52

figure 4.1

professional and technical occupations are growing rapidly

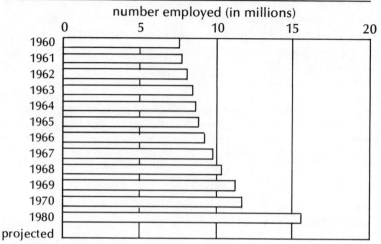

number employed (in millions)

Source: *Jobs for the 1970's: Slide Series* (Washington, D.C.: U.S. Department of Labor, Bureau of Labor Statistics, 1971), p. 22.

but it is probable that there will be an overproduction of many Ph.D. and professionally trained people.[8] DeWitt and Tussing estimate that some 400,000 doctorates will be awarded during the 1970s and warn that should the doctorate recipients be employed in government, academia and industry at the same rate as in the immediate past, approximately one-half of those produced can expect employment. They expect, however, that there will be a much greater demand for most Ph.D.'s in government and industry than in the past and that Ph.D.'s will be hired to do jobs that could be done by individuals with a lesser amount of training.[9]

In his study for the Bureau of Labor Statistics, Rosenthal concluded that, although there may be shortages and oversupplies in some areas, ". . . the supply and demand for college graduates as a whole is expected to be in relative balance during the 1970's."[10]

training idea people

Table 4.1 reports an overall summary of the employment prospects for college-educated people. In developing the data in this table, demand includes growth, replacement due to death and retirement, and other reasons for leaving the labor force. Basic assumptions related to data in Table 4.1 are:

1. The fundamental structure of the nation's economy will not change sharply in the 1970s.

table 4.1

occupational employment, 1968 and project requirements, 1980, for college graduates

occupation	estimated 1968 employment	projected 1980 requirements	percent change	supply estimated to be
chemists	130,000	200,000	55.7	significantly
counselors	71,000	107,000	49.8	below re-
dietitians	30,000	42,000	40.3	quirements
dentists	100,000	130,000	31.7	
physicians	295,000	450,000	53.1	
physicists	45,000	75,000	63.9	
engineers	1,100,00	1,500,000	40.2	slightly short
geologists and geophysicists	30,000	36,000	20.6	of require- ments
optometrists	17,000	21,000	23.5	
architects	34,000	50,000	47.1	in balance
lawyers	270,000	335,000	22.7	with require- ments
pharmacists	121,000	130,000	7.0	slightly above re- quirements
mathematicians	70,000	110,000	60.5	significantly
life scientists	168,000	238,000	40.8	above re-
teachers, elementary and secondary	2,170,000	2,340,000	7.8	quirements

Source: *College Educated Workers, 1968-1980* (Washington, D.C.: U.S. Department of Labor, 1970), p. 1.

2. By 1980 there will be full employment, meaning an unemployment rate between 3 and 4 percent.

3. The United States will not be fighting a war and defense spending will be reduced.

4. Military personnel will be reduced to a pre-Vietnam level.

5. High quality of environment values will be continued.

6. Manpower policies and a growth economy will be stabilized.

7. More federal funds will be shared at state and local levels.

Assumptions underlying Rosenthal's supply study are:

1. Differential occupational status will continue to motivate people to enter jobs differentially.

2. A continually increasing proportion of the college-age population will attend college.

3. Current trends in subjects studied by college students will continue.

4. Current trends for other than U.S. college graduates to enter various occupations will continue. These entrants will include immigrants, up-graded workers and labor force reentrants.[11]

As our urbanized society grows and matures, opportunites for highly trained specialists will continue to expand both quantitatively and qualitatively as automation and cybernation tend to reduce other types of work. As America moves into the twenty-first century, the need for work with the mind will be increased both technologically and aesthetically and will be directed toward improving the quality of life for the individual. Therefore, specialized training for the benefit of individuals and for society as a whole is examined in the following pages in some considerable detail.

high school training

High school training, almost by definition, in the urbanized society is preparatory training. For the large number of college-bound high school students, the course of study is generally preparatory idea training. High school graduates totaled 1,971,000 in 1960-61, 3,036,000 in 1970-71 and they are expected to total some 3,340,000 in 1980-81.[12]

junior college training

More than just passing reference must be made to junior colleges. While these schools have not primarily trained idea people, their numbers have increased so much in recent years that they must be reviewed as a source of preparatory training for specialists. Between 1960 and 1970 enrollment in degree programs offered by two-year institutions increased from 451,335 to 1,629,982. Their enrollment is projected to increase to 3,001,000 by 1980.[13] This enrollment increase was slightly more than twice the degree enrollment in four-year colleges. By 1968-69 there were almost 1,000 junior colleges in operation, while in 1961 there were only 678.

In years past, most students who attended junior colleges eventually transferred to four-year institutions. By 1968 the proportion for planned transfer had dropped to approximately 60 percent. Junior and community colleges are increasingly providing two-year, career-oriented training. Most junior colleges still maintain a two-year transfer or liberal arts program, but most students enter the two-year career programs. In 1968 the largest number of graduates majored in business studies, followed by mechanical and engineering technology, drafting, construction, metallurgy, auto mechanics, electronics, and instrumentation. Other important programs are medical technology, dental assistance and dental hygiene, radiology, library technology, and police-officer training.

Most of the training offered by the junior colleges is funded through local agencies and most students come from local areas. Neither the level of instruction nor the social class of junior college students are typical training centers for idea people. Most idea people who were trained in junior colleges transferred to senior colleges to complete advanced training.

Nevertheless, as junior colleges enroll more students and as the demand for technical skills increases, the potential expands for further idea training in the junior colleges.

college training

The three unique orientations of higher education in the United States combined to stimulate the preparation of idea people. In terms of both function and operation, much American higher education can be separated into these categories: instruction, research, and public service.[14] In effect the university is a place for knowledge generation through its research programs, a place for knowledge dissemination through instruction, and a place for application of ideas in the real world. This triple focus originated in the land-grant state universities in 1862. Since then, in varying degrees, many older private and public institutions of higher learning have opted for this three pronged educational focus, which has come to dominate the North American University.

The four-year college degree has been the primary traditional training ground for idea people. In 1891 the president of Harvard University suggested that the baccalaureate degree be awarded in three years. The suggestion was overwhelmingly defeated by the Harvard faculty.[15] With the exception of this alternate suggestion, the four-year model became firmly established in the nineteenth century and until recently has held steadily. Recently the Carnegie Commission on Higher Education issued a report titled *Less Time, More Options*. This report, in essence, called for three-year degree programs. As idea training becomes more prevalent and as ideas proliferate, there will be even more pressure to hasten early training and follow it with various patterns of continuous training throughout one's career. Shortened degree programs facilitate the shift from acquiring all knowledge before starting a career. Although there are complaints that a shortened degree program will mean a cheapened degree, nevertheless, most schools are moving in various ways to shortened degrees.

training idea people

Some of the three-year models involve giving credit by demonstrating knowledge and expertise by examination. Others are suggesting a four-year program with three years of study on campus and one year of off-campus work. At Princeton a proposal is being made not only to shorten the time for undergraduate education but also to modify the school calendar into trimesters of eleven, six, and eleven weeks rather than twelve-week semesters. The purpose of such a modification is to recognize that all courses should not have intellectual parity expressed by the same number of weeks of study. This is a further innovation which will facilitate idea training in the college environment.

The proposed Princeton Plan suggests most clearly a direction for optimum idea training. If career goals are clearly expressed by students, the amount of training opportunity for optimum achievement can be appropriately both shortened and extended in the interest of quality training.

While the focus in this chapter is almost exclusively on idea training, this is in no way to overlook the fact that a considerable amount of undergraduate college and university education is not idea people training as such. Many students may want to take numerous electives outside of or beyond those courses which are primary to career training. These and other options which in appropirate cases might enhance idea training should be facilitated.

financing higher education

In 1966-67 the total expenditures for higher education were estimated to be approximately $12 billion.[16] At that time the distribution for current expenditures was: instruction, $6.0 billion; research, $2.5 billion; public service, $1.0 billion; auxiliary service, $2.0 billion; student aid, $0.5 million. For the same year current operating income was $12.2 billion, which was distributed as follows: charges, $5.0 billion; government, $6.2 billion; state government $3.0 billion; federal government, $2.9 billion; endowment, $4.0 million; gifts, $6.0 million. Two important points are clear from these figures. First, half of the current operating budget is expended for instruction. This includes more than idea people preparation. Secondly, half of current income is supplied by governments, divided approximately equally between state and federal. Charges make up almost half of the operating expenditures with philanthropy being a significant but proportionally small source. These data clearly indicate that colleges as training centers for idea people are significantly supported by state and federal governments.

The expenditures for 1970-71 and the anticipated expenditures for 1980-81 are shown in Table 4.2. In the 1970s higher education expenditures are anticipated to increase from $24.2 billion to $43.8 billion. The total expenditure for student education will rise from $14.8 billion to $37.3 billion. Organized research will increase from $2.6 billion to $4.4 billion. No single statistic makes it more clear that the first function of higher education is training, while the second function is research or the production of new knowledge. Auxiliary enterprises actually constitute the second largest amount of money allocation, but they are exactly what the name implies—auxiliary and not a primary function of higher education. It may well be that by 1980 a larger proportion of funding will go to idea production and research in universities and/or other agencies. As automation and cybernation become more characteristic of American society, environmental quality and gratification will lie more in idea creativeness.

In recent years there has been increased federal support for higher education. The 1973 budget was $7.4 billion, while $7 billion was allocated for the preceding fiscal year. There have been various shifts of focus in the federal funding of higher education as the government has sought to provide leadership as well as dollars to areas of national relevance. For example, the 1973 budget provided less support for physical facilities and an increased emphasis on student aid, particularly for the disadvantaged.

The $7.4 billion in federal funding for higher education is about 20 percent of the total cost of U.S. higher education

table 4.2
higher education expenditures (in billions of 1970-71 dollars)

	1970-71	1980-81
total expenditures from current funds	$24.2	$43.8
public institutions	15.4	20.2
student education	10.0	20.2
organized research	1.5	2.5
related activities	0.5	0.9
auxiliary enterprises	1.9	3.5
student aid	0.6	1.6
major public service	0.9	1.6
private institutions	8.8	13.5
student education	4.8	7.0
organized research	1.1	1.9
related activities	0.2	0.4
auxiliary enterprises	1.4	2.0
student aid	0.6	1.1
major public service	0.7	1.1
capital outlay, current funds	0.7	0.3

Source: *The Chronicle of Higher Education,* 6 (April 17, 1972), p. 1.

during fiscal 1973. During the preceding fiscal year it has been estimated that the federal government supplied 25 percent of the cost of higher education. Most of the government's allocation of funds to higher education is through the Office of Education. In addition significant funding through other HEW programs in areas like health are provided for higher education. Also significant amounts of money for higher education are allocated through agency programs like the following: veterans' education and training, almost $2 billion; National Science Foundation over $650 million; Agricultural Extension Service $181 million; Agricultural Cooperative Research, approximately $87 million; and Arts and Humanities Foundation, almost $83 million.

The education of idea people at the graduate and professional levels is the most expensive training in America. Moreover, projections indicate that in the 1970s the cost of graduate education will exceed all others. The cost of graduate education may reach an annual rate of $20 billion, plus a $3 billion physical plant expenditure, by 1980. These projections take into account inflation and increased research.[17] Most higher education is already public rather than private. It is projected that enrollments during the 1970s will increase more than twice as rapidly at public than at private colleges and universities.[18]

Junior colleges are being given proportionately higher rates of federal support than senior colleges in recent years, and only a small part of this training is at the idea people level.

faculties

Faculties are a major element of the academic community. They are idea disseminators and, to a considerable extent, idea producers. Until recently, college and university faculties have held a near monopoly on instruction. With the increasing complexity of urbanized society, a greater need for on-the-job and off-campus training has developed. In juxtaposition there is more need for off-campus personnel to be employed as at least temporary trainers of on-campus people. In effect specialized training in contemporary society is going beyond university faculty and campuses as relevant knowledge and resources can no longer be sufficiently maintained only on campuses.

In traditional academic communities the department is the key unit for research and training. Departments are in effect controllers of specialized bodies of knowledge and the units within which specialists function. They developed out of nineteenth- and early twentieth-century college and societal needs. With the knowledge explosion and the proliferation of experts and specialists in totally new bodies of knowledge, earlier specialties are being expanded, eroded, and in some cases replaced. Accordingly, universities have organized "centers" and "institutes" which focus on multidisciplinary and interdisciplinary instruction, research, and the generating of public service. Idea people are, for example, no longer just engineers, but aerospace engineers; no longer just chemists, but physical chemists; no longer just psychologists, but social psychologists; no longer just business majors, but systems experts and so forth. Totally new bodies of knowledge and various forms of integrations of older bodies of knowledge are widespread.

Subjects of training and research are further organized into colleges and/or schools. These too have come to maintain boundaries which, for contemporary needs, often become excessively constraining. Colleges and schools are modifying their boundaries and focus to recognize and give leadership in developing new directions. Agricultural schools, for example, are becoming schools of environmental sciences; schools of home economics are becoming schools of family and social living; schools of architecture are becoming architecture and planning schools, and so forth. Some totally new schools are being established in the areas of urban studies and planning and environmental sciences. In effect, the basic structures of colleges and universities are being greatly modified and re-oriented for preparing specialists to work in these new areas. International studies and on-site area studies are ascending in importance as idea people further wrestle with the world as their place of work rather than a smaller geopolitical sub-division. Men and environment subjects are ascending in importance as matters of pollution become more plaguing. Sea-grant colleges have been established by the federal government as component units of existing colleges to stimulate research, exploration and training of idea people in areas of environmental concern. Similarly, in the 1973 federal budget for higher education, more funds will be made available for higher education, more funds will be made available for the health sciences and for health training facilities and centers. This is another effort on the part of the federal government to exercise directional leadership in the area of idea research, training, and public service.

growth of colleges and universities

In the second half of the twentieth century, the growth of new colleges and universities at the four-year level and above has been steady.[19] Much of this expansion has been supported by state governments. As states compete to provide quality of environments for their citizens, their leaders have become increasingly aware of the importance of post-high-school education. This is more than saying that going to college has become a "vogue." Investment in higher education not only contributes to support for idea people but also contributes to quality of environment for citizens generally.

With increasing needs for idea people, both new junior and senior colleges are being established. Because most senior colleges enroll a majority of their students from a two hundred-mile radius,[20] it has been asserted that senior colleges should be in or close to metropolitan centers. In such centers it is probable that the minimum student enrollment should be no less than five thousand to obtain quality training.

The cost of financing higher education for idea people varies greatly with subject matter and instructional methods. Different emphasis may be placed on the use of large classes, programmed learning, televised instruction, independent study, and so forth. Differential student-faculty ratios sharply influence costs for training. Similarly, the costs are influenced by salary rates, amounts of office space, research facilities, library, size of classes, and support material.[21] There are significant fund source differentials between public and private institutions.[22]

undergraduate scientist training

It is found that students who are most likely to pursue science careers after college are those who started as science or engineering majors, whose aptitude is high, and whose like-sexed parent has a higher than average education.[23] Further it is reported that Northeastern men's colleges produce fewer graduates who ultimately obtain the Ph.D. degree than is expected on the basis of intelligence and other socioeconomic characteristics. Technological institutions tend to have a positive effect on the later production of scientists and co-educational liberal arts colleges have some positive effect on male students moving into careers in science.[24]

aspirations of college seniors

The training environment of idea people is influenced by the professional trainers, and by the aspirations of students. Student aspirations are influenced by peer groups, families, and societal structures. When good paying jobs are clearly the reward for more higher education, this societal structure, often bolstered by peer groups and families, has in the urbanized society traditionally encouraged more people to pursue advanced training. Accordingly, such structural guidelines in the 1950s and 1960s moved a large number of students to aspire beyond baccalaureate degrees for master's and Ph.D. degrees. With the contraction of employment opportunities anticipated in the 1970s and 1980s, a smaller number of students may seek higher levels of training.

A profile of 1961 college graduates included the following: more men than women, age in their early twenties, from families with several children, predominately white, predominately urban, and predominately middle class. Furthermore the parents had at least graduated from high school and were managers or professionals with annual income over $7,500. The graduates themselves had worked part-time during the latter part of college. Their religion was typically Protestant.[25]

An overwhelmingly large proportion of the college seniors aspired to graduate study. In terms of the Academic Performance Index (API) a high achievement was the most important factor in positively influencing plans for further study. The increasing proportion of students aged 18-24 enrolled in college reveals their enlarged impact on idea employment. Their proportion was 14 percent in 1950, 22 percent in 1960 and 32 percent in 1970.[26] Similarly, in the period prior to the 1920s less than a thousand Ph.D.s were granted each year and by 1960 the number was nearly 10,000 and by 1970 the number was 29,872. In the Davis study almost 33 percent of the June,

1961, graduates planned to attend graduate or professional school in the fall of that year. An additional nearly 45 percent planned to attend graduate or professional schools after 1961-62, though they did not specify a particular year. Indeed less than 23 percent of the total 56,664 students studied did not plan to pursue advanced post-graduate study.[27] Put another way, over three-quarters of the June 1961 graduates anticipated post-graduate study at some future date. This is a larger proportion of college graduates anticipating graduate study than of high school graduates anticipating undergraduate college study. Or in the vernacular, "if everybody plans to go college now," it is similarly apparent that "everybody with a college degree plans to take an advanced degree."

Most advanced or post-graduate degrees are occupationally specific. They constitute idea people training at its most focused point. Moreover, with such depth in occupational training, there is limited flexibility for the post-graduate trained person to shift from one occupation to another and effectively use his investment and society's investment in him. Baccalaureate-level people are often trained more generally and can, accordingly, be more flexible in their career development. For individual satisfaction, manpower planning and societal equilibrium, careful projections ought to be made and utilized for expanding and contracting post-graduate study. In spite of the frequent criticism that American higher education is excessively career oriented, some 67 percent of the students in the Davis study responded that their undergraduate training was basic general education. Only 32 percent indicated that they were specifically involved in career training.[28]

graduate and professional training

There is some shifting focus from arts training to professional fields as advanced career experiences are anticipated. Thirty-eight percent of the Davis study respondents had majored in arts and science subjects as undergraduates. Also thirty percent anticipated graduate study in the arts and science field (namely, physics, social sciences, chemistry, other physical sciences, mathematics, biological sciences, and the humanities), but only 18 percent anticipated a career in the arts and sciences. Forty-five percent had majored in professional fields as undergraduates (namely, education, engineering, pre-law, pre-medicine, social work, and other professional fields). Fifty-seven percent anticipated graduate study in professional fields and 59 percent anticipated careers in professional fields. Fifteen percent had majored in business administration or agriculture. Only 12 percent anticipated continued study in business or agriculture and only 20 percent anticipated professional careers in these areas.

In terms of manpower planning and idea people training, it is of great significance that only 20 percent of the undergraduate students anticipate continuing their post-graduate study immediately. The median age for receiving the Ph.D. is thirty. Increasingly the trend for retirement is age sixty-five or earlier. Accordingly, this highly trained, highly talented and expensive manpower has on the average little more than thirty years of full productivity, for individual satisfaction and for service to society. In the technical areas, where significant intellectual production surfaces between the late twenties and early thirties, it appears that the time lag for training reduces much potential high-talent creativity.[29] In effect this maximizes high-talent "waste."

Bayers finds that students ranking high on the Academic Performance Index (API) disproportionally plan to continue their post-graduate education immediately, while the lower-ranking API students manifest numerous direct and indirect reasons for their procrastination. Women are much less likely to continue their training immediately regardless of high API ratings, choice of career field, or marital status.

The primary purpose of graduate and professional schools is specialized professional training. In the United States this kind of advanced training began in 1861 when Yale University offered the first American Ph.D. This level of training grew continuously but slowly for many years. In the 1930s only forty-five universities granted as many as 10 Ph.D.s a year.[30] By the 1960s over 16,000 Ph.D. degrees were being granted annually. From 1861 through 1970 over 340,000 Ph.D. degrees had been awarded by North American universities, half of these degrees being awarded in the decade of the 1960s. If current trends continue, projections indicate that by 1980 between 369,000 and 520,000 new Ph.D. degrees will be awarded.[31] The Council of Graduate Schools reports over two hundred institutions now offering graduate degrees. The eligible number of potential undergraduates for graduate schools is increasing sharply. For example, in 1965 some 530,000 students received bachelor's degrees. It is projected that by 1980 bachelor's degrees will be awarded to 1,333,000 students.[32] The number of doctorates projected for 1980 range widely but as high as 68,700 (see Table 4.3).

table 4.3
higher education earned degrees

	1970-71	1980-81*
bachelor's and first profession	863,000	1,334,000
natural sciences	188,860	257,200
math, statistics	29,940	44,000
engineering	44,650	48,530
physical sciences	21,180	26,440
biological sciences	38,460	55,630
agriculture, forestry	13,100	18,410
health professions	37,790	60,510
general science	3,110	3,680
social sciences, humanities	674,140	1,075,800
fine arts	59,710	98,650
English, journalism	64,970	100,860
foreign languages	21,840	34,530
psychology	36,930	78,890
social sciences	166,010	306,070
education	136,650	184,120
library science	1,110	1,810
social work	4,690	13,560

training idea people

table 4.3 (continued)

	1970-71	1980-81*
business and commerce	116,480	164,400
other	66,050	92,910
master's	224,000	395,900
natural sciences	44,060	70,860
math, statistics	7,770	13,420
engineering	15,670	24,050
physical sciences	5,940	8,720
biological sciences	6,240	10,650
agriculture, forestry	2,530	3,580
health professions	4,910	8,730
general science	1,000	1,710
social sciences, humanities	179,940	325,040
fine arts	14,210	25,060
English, journalism	10,000	17,810
foreign languages	5,420	9,730
psychology	4,820	8,270
social sciences	20,500	38,200
education	77,190	128,270
library science	7,120	13,130
social work	5,850	9,040
business and commerce	26,270	60,530
other	8,560	15,000
doctor's	32,000	68,700
natural sciences	14,650	26,060
math, statistics	1,480	3,230
engineering	3,820	6,100
physical sciences	4,440	7,170
biological sciences	3,540	6,590
agriculture, forestry	940	2,000
health professions	400	900
general science	30	70
social sciences, humanities	17,350	42,640
fine arts	1,120	2,660
English, journalism	1,310	2,510
foreign languages	1,010	1,880
psychology	1,740	4,210
social sciences	3,960	8,510
education	6,210	18,380

table 4.3 (concluded)

	1970-71	1980-81*
library science	40	80
social work	100	230
business and commerce	760	2,130
other	1,100	2,050

Source: *The Chronicle of Higher Education* 6 (April 17, 1972), p. 1.
*Estimated.

graduate school expansion

There are several major historical dates in the development of graduate education in the United States. Some master's-level work was started in 1642 and phased out approximately one hundred years later. Research doctoral degrees were awarded in Europe in 1817. Master's degree work was initiated in America for a second time in 1856, followed by doctoral research work in 1861. With the passing of the act to establish the land-grant colleges in 1862, graduate education was moved rapidly forward with federal initiative. In 1887 more federal support was provided for academic research in agriculture. In 1946 a widespread general federal support was provided for academic research, and from 1950 to the late 1960s federal support for graduate education has increased.[33]

From 1861 when the first Ph.D. was offered in the United States, there have been three major periods of graduate education expansion. The first of these occurred between 1921 and 1931 with an expansion of annual number of doctorates earned from some 650 to 2,500. In 1921 less than sixty universities awarded this highest academic degree and by 1931 an additional eighteen had been added to that distinguished category.[34] The second period of graduate education expansion occurred after World War II. Just prior to the war the annual number of earned doctorates was over 3,000. During the war years it dropped to less than 2,000, and by 1954 earned doctorates had increased sharply to 9,000. With this period of expansion, the number of schools offering the Ph.D. degree increased to well over 100. The third period of expansion was

training idea people

from 1962 to 1972. In the early 1960s the annual number of earned doctorates was approximately 11,500 and a decade later, in 1970, it was 29,436. The number of schools awarding the top academic degree had now increased to approximately 200. Graduate school enrollments are projected to expand from 315,000 in 1960 to approximately 1,000,000 by 1975.[35]

Where these Ph.D.'s will obtain employment is a matter of considerable concern and speculation, but some observers submit that supply creates its own demand. When some half century ago the nation extended its free education to the twelfth grade, there was a concern that there would be insufficient jobs for high school graduates. And immediately following World War II there was concern that there would be an insufficient number of jobs for college graduates, when approximately 20 percent of high school graduates were going to college. As the knowledge base and the need for new skills expanded in American society, both high school and college graduates have been readily absorbed into the labor force.[36]

Another important characteristic in the expansion of graduate education is the shift from a few schools to many in this training. As recently as 1925 fifteen universities awarded 75 percent of the nation's doctorates. By 1934 these same universities awarded only 60 percent of the doctorates, by 1950 only 50 percent, and by the middle 1960s less than 40 percent. If the present trends continue, by 1980 the originally few dominant universities will award fewer than 20 percent of the highest academic degrees.[37] Indeed by 1980, with the present trend, over three hundred universities will be awarding an average of ten or more doctorate degrees annually. Another one hundred universities will award fewer than ten Ph.D.'s each year, making a grand total of approximately four hundred awarding the highest academic degree. With this massive expansion of graduate education, old prestigious schools are being challenged both qualitatively and quantitatively.[38]

In the decade of the 1960s some 60 percent of the new doctorates obtained their first post-doctoral positions in higher education. In the 1970s it is anticipated that 25 percent or less will be needed for employment in higher education.[39] From 1971 to 1980, between three hundred thousand and five hundred thousand new doctorates are expected. The Office of Education projects that some 56 percent will be in the area of science and engineering, including mathematics and social sciences. In education the number of doctorate degrees, both the Ph.D. and Ed.D., is increasing rapidly. Between 1966 and 1971 some twenty-seven thousand doctorates were earned in education. Between 1950 and 1965 only twenty-four thousand doctorates were earned in education, and it is projected that between 1971 and 1980 approximately eighty thousand new doctorates in education will be awarded. They will seek to become teachers and administrators at all levels, and many of them will be frustrated by lack of expansion, if not contraction, of opportunities due to declining enrollments through 1980. Indeed college enrollments (of persons between the late teens and early twenties) are expected to increase only slightly through 1982 and then decline until about 1988 after which the magnitude of the upswing will be related to the new birth rate.[40] College enrollments for individuals thirty and over should increase precipitously from now to the end of the century.

Earning the doctoral degree is expensive in time as well as in money. There is an over eight-year median time period for persons in all fields to complete the doctoral degree; five of those years are actually spent in residence working for the degree. The greatest amount of time elapse is in education— about fourteen years. Professional areas such as business, religion, and home economics require about ten years, while the physical sciences typically demand the least number of years—slightly more than six.

In the United States in 1964 there were approximately 265 graduate students for each 100,000 population. The range was from 1,563 in the District of Columbia to only 50 in Maine. Seven major eastern states had graduate enrollments well above the national average, while only five eastern states had enrollments considerably below the national average. If idea people are to serve the nation as a whole and not just the eastern part of the nation, it is increasingly critical that qualitative and quantitative training be offered throughout the nation. There is considerable evidence that much of the impact of idea people is directly related to their personal and professional interaction with local populations. While idea people themselves are very career mobile, their total impact tends to be made in local areas and thereby justifies considerable dispersion of training centers.[41] From this perspective many states have a considerable deficiency in graduate enrollment in order to bring their training up to the national average.

Recruitment into advanced training. Throughout the twentieth century occupational opportunities for idea people have been expanding in America. In a success- and achievement-oriented society, the disproportionately high degree of prestige and remuneration of professionals have been sufficient to recruit the large number of people needed. The professional and executive managerial categories in American society are still the most rapidly growing groups, even though at a lower rate than in the immediate past. There are a number of studies concerning recruitment of individuals into graduate and professional training. There has been some examination to determine when undergraduates decide to continue their education, how it is implemented after such a decision has been reached, and the extent of student awareness of scholarships and other assistance.[42]

The prestige-salary mechanism for recruitment has generally worked satisfactorily as indicated by Davie's finding that some 77 percent of the nation's seniors in 1961 planned to attend graduate or professional school. Over 30 percent anticipated continuing directly by matriculating in the fall of 1961-62. There were significant regional variations with the 1961 findings reporting plans for continued graduate or professional education the immediately following year as follows: New England-Middle Atlantic, 39 percent; North Central, 31 percent; Mountains Pacific, 31 percent; and South-South Central, 21 percent. Grigg's study in the South makes it clear that the ". . . level of education of the parents, particularly the father, appeared to be a more important socioeconomic factor than either income or occupation"[43] in determining who actually continued graduate and professional education immediately following their undergraduate work.

In addition to the student's general orientation to graduate study, whether or not a student is accepted into a graduate program is influenced greatly by grade-point averages, standing in one's class, and Graduate Record Examination scores. Added to these so-called "objective" measures are autobiographical statements expressing the applicant's career goals and personal interviews.[44] Over the years this recruitment pattern has generated students who are "the very model of their faculty" and, indeed, largely white, Anglo-Saxon, Protestant. More recently universities, professional schools, foundations, and the federal government have placed increasing priority on recruiting minority students into graduate and professional education. Priority has also been placed on recruiting female professionals and graduate students. In the latter case by the mid-1960s females constituted approximately one-half of the baccalaureate degree recipients but only 11 percent of the doctoral recipients.[45]

By the 1970s three-fourths of the graduate faculty studied by Heiss reported satisfaction with recruitment and admissions procedures. Furthermore almost 60 percent of the graduate faculty indicated they expected the admission requirements to remain approximately the same for the foreseeable future.

One of the more significant problem areas with recruitment and admission currently centers around full-time versus part-time students. With major graduate and professional schools increasingly located in major metropolitan areas, there are more opportunities for students to be employed full time and study part time. There is considerable question in academia concerning the satisfactory performance of part-time students. Some departments heavily oppose part-time students and others, apparently with equal vigor, recruit them. In spite of

training idea people

this debate, slightly more than half of the graduate faculty expect the supply of well-qualified applicants in their fields to increase over the next several years.

The other side of recruitment is attrition. Attrition rates are high—estimated to run about 30 percent in top-ranked universities and as high as 50 percent in other graduate schools.[46] While the dropouts from Ph.D. programs are not necessarily lost to idea-oriented occupations, from a manpower planning and policy point of view, as well as from a training point of view, a high attrition rate is costly both to individuals and to society. The high economic and social cost to individuals and society for partial training ought to be reduced by more careful and satisfactory screening of applicants. Also the sociopsychological frustration to individuals who do not complete the course of study is great. Business leaders may look upon education as a new "growth industry." Graduate school deans and department chairpersons may be committed to society's need for more highly trained individuals, but nevertheless, the quality and quantity of training could be focused more by a reduction in attrition rates. Part of this reduction should be achieved by examining student criticism of the failure on the part of training institutions and faculty to orient new students and potential students adequately. There is much aura and mystique about getting a Ph.D. in the graduate schools. Graduate catalogues and other related materials are criticized for providing insufficient information concerning the requirements for achievement at this high level. Much attrition is, therefore, associated with disillusion which could be avoided by making more explicit the nature of the study and the detailed requirements before people enter.

graduate student attitudes concerning their training

A recent survey shows graduate students to be serious idea people, seeking knowledge to serve society and to improve it through responsible activity.[47] Students express the attitude that they are in graduate school to: serve mankind better, 76 percent; contribute to societal change, 60 percent; increase their earning power, 81 percent; satisfy job requirements, 67 percent; continue intellectual growth, 95 percent; prepare for academic career, 66 percent; and study for the intrinsic interest of the field, 73 percent. Over three-fourths of the graduate students report satisfaction with the education they are getting, yet 38 percent indicate that much of what is taught is irrelevant. Sixty percent believe that departmental graduate programs favor bright students, 84 percent believe that faculty members should be free to present any idea in class, and only 36 percent believe that genuine scholarship is threatened by big research centers.

Idea people have a history of considerable mobility. Only about half of the graduate students indicated that they planned to stay in the same state after they completed their graduate education. In terms of study environment 70 percent indicated that disruptive students should be expelled or suspended. Sixty percent believed that most college officials are too lax on student protest. Over three-quarters of the graduate students believed that they should not control decision making in respect to faculty appointments and promotion, departmental graduate admission policy, and advanced degree requirements. Forty-six percent believed that they should have more responsibility for revision and content of graduate courses. Also 66 percent indicated that a strike may at sometimes be a legitimate faculty action, and 60 percent indicated that a strike may sometimes be a legitimate action by teaching assistants.

graduate student characteristics

The American Council on Education data reported by Creager reveals a continuing sex bias, with 66 percent of the students being male. Ethnically 93 percent of graduate students are Caucasian. Forty-seven percent of graduate students are between the ages of twenty-six and thirty-nine, and 25 percent between the ages of twenty-six and twenty-nine. Sixty-one percent are married. Their primary source of income since entering graduate school is: fellowship, 14 percent; assistantship, 22 percent; nonacademic job, 20 percent; spouse's job,

17 percent; savings, 4 percent; investments, 0.8 percent; aid from family, 8 percent; personal loan, 0.5 percent; governmental or institutional loan, 3.5 percent; other, 9 percent.

In terms of graduate student religious orientation, 51 percent responded that they were moderately religious, 30 percent largely indifferent, 12 percent deeply religious, and 7 percent basically opposed. Indeed, when asked about present religious affiliation, 23 percent indicated none. Nineteen percent were Roman Catholic, 10 percent Jewish, 8 percent Methodist, 6 percent Presbyterian, 5 percent Episcopalian, and the others ranged widely. Forty-nine percent were full-time students, 39 percent part-time students, and 12 percent currently not enrolled. Forty-nine percent responded that their institution was a very good place, 45 percent a fairly good place, and 6 percent that it was not an appropriate place for them.

Students evaluated the following as good or excellent: ability of fellow students, 70 percent; achievement of faculty, 77 percent; variety of courses, 49 percent; availability of faculty to graduate students, 61 percent; classroom instruction, 52 percent; relevance of course for future occupation, 59 percent; intellectual environment, 55 percent; academic reputation of department, 66 percent; personal relations with other graduate students, 76.

Their undergraduate grade average was: A or A+, 6.9 percent; A−, 14 percent; B+, 22 percent; B, 19 percent; B−, 19 percent; C+, 15 percent; C, or below 3 percent. The time devoted per week for studying was: none, 4.5 percent; 1-4 hours, 19 percent; 5-8 hours, 16 percent; 9-12 hours, 13 percent; 13-20 hours, 16 percent; 21-30 hours, 14 percent; 31-40 hours, 9 percent; and over 40 hours, 8 percent. Hours spent in laboratories were: none, 15 percent; 1-4 hours, 26 percent; 5-8 hours, 20 percent; 9-12 hours, 17 percent; 13-20 hours, 13 percent; 21-31 hours, 4 percent; 21-40 hours, 3 percent; and over 40 hours, 2 percent. Over 70 percent of the graduate students attend professional meetings. In terms of career expectation 28 percent anticipated university teaching, 14 percent expected elementary or secondary teaching, 12 percent anticipated professional practice, 14 percent expected executive or administrative employment, 5 percent anticipated junior college employment, 6 percent anticipated research in industry, and 7 percent expected professional self employment, with the remaining proportion in a range of jobs.

master's-level training

Master's degrees, like doctoral degrees, have a long history and one which means different things to different people in different times and places. The awarding of master's degrees is increasing. In 1962-63 nearly 88,000 earned master's degrees were awarded in the United States. By 1970-71 the number of earned master's degrees was 224,000.[48]

The master's degree has, in effect, two histories in the United States. Prior to the 1860s several universities including Harvard, New York University (then the University of the City of New York), Columbia, the University of Virginia, and the University of Michigan attempted, unsuccessfully, to establish a master's program. Starting in the 1870s the second effort was made to establish the master's-level training. From that time to the present it has succeeded. In 1961-62 some 621 schools awarded some type of master's degree.[49] In the early 1960s master's degrees were awarded by 143 universities, 218 liberal arts colleges, 122 teachers colleges, 28 technical schools, 59 theological and religious institutions, 26 schools of art, and 25 other professional schools. This array of institutions offering master's degrees makes it clear that it is both liberal arts and professional. In the early 1960s considerable regional differences were reported in the awarding of master's degrees. Thirty-four percent were awarded in the East, 30 percent in the Midwest, 18 percent in the South, and 17 percent in the Far West.[50]

For many individuals the earning of a master's degree is part of the process of earning a Ph.D. One-fourth of the Ph.D.-training departments also require students to earn the master's degree. Most people who earn a Ph.D. degree also earn a

training idea people

master's degree, but the reverse is not true.[51] The awarding of master's degrees varies greatly by field. In 1970-71 master's degrees awarded by field were: education, 77,190; engineering, 15,670; social science, 20,500; business and commerce, 26,270; physical sciences, 5,940; English and journalism, 10,000; fine arts, 14,210; mathematics, 7,770; biological sciences, 6,240; psychology, 4,820; foreign languages, 5,420; agriculture, 2,530; health professions, 4,910; general science, 1,000; social work, 5,805; library sciences, 7,120; and other 8,560.[52] The master's degree is a terminal professional degree in many subject areas, and it is increasingly important in junior college teaching. To some extent it is used temporarily for positions in four-year colleges as well.

With the various challenges and pressures to train more idea people at appropriate levels, the master's degree is continually expanding and being modified. In some cases attention is given to the development of a so-called three-year master's degree, where the last two years in undergraduate school and one year following are systematically planned for more intensified and professional type training.[53]

From 1970-71 to 1980-81 the number of baccalaureate and first professional degrees will increase from 863,000 to an estimated 1,334,000. For the same time period the number of master's degrees will increase from 224,000 to an estimated 395,900. Similarly for doctoral degrees the increase will be from 32,000 to 68,700. Table 4.3 (pages 67-69) indicates the respective number and anticipated increase by discipline.[54]

"real world" idea people training

Due to the abstract nature of advanced training, the basics or fundamentals are most adequately disseminated on university campuses. On the other hand, much idea training becomes oriented to application in the real world. Training that is applicable to the real world is most relevant when off-campus sites are utilized as part of the learning environment. In the late 1960s American corporations were spending annually more to train their employees than the combined budgets of colleges and universities, at that time approximately $13 to $14 billion.[55] Although much corporation training is below the level of the highly specialized and skilled, some corporations train their own specialists because institutions of higher learning are unable or unwilling to orient their courses sufficiently to societal relevance. A considerable amount of corporate training is financed at federal expense, primarily through special corporate tax structures.[56]

In some cases relevant and intellectually stimulating post-doctoral training is found in nonuniversity laboratories. Both government and private laboratories are included, for example, Rand Corporation, Bell Telephone Laboratories, DuPont Laboratories, and General Electric Laboratories. In the public sector NASA, the National Institutes of Health, the U.S. Department of Agriculture Experiment Stations, and so forth all constitute significant places for advanced study.

Increasingly in the social sciences and professional areas, off-campus training is required. One of the oldest precedents for this model of training is in medicine, where the young physicians become hospital interns. In recent years practitionerships or practicums of numerous types have been considered desirable and, where possible, have been required in other areas of study. Much doctoral dissertation research requires off-campus on-location study. In the areas of city planning and urban studies, urban observatories are established to follow the on-campus study of theory and methods. For many years professional educators have used schools as laboratories for training purposes. Several major universities with outstanding engineering programs have developed off-campus but tangentially attached research and development facilities which in part are used for advanced study. Although some of these have come under critical attack by students, faculty, and administrators for their engagement in classified research, it is clear that these programs have been instituted to seek greater relevancy in professional training. These programs also illustrate some of the major difficulties in making advanced training relevant.

educational social space for idea people

The place of specialized training on the scale of social priorities can be illustrated in several ways. Three of the most clear indicators are: budget for higher education, number of students, and the public versus private school distribution of students and funds. Viewed from any of these perspectives, the importance which society places on higher education, and the amount of specialized and professional training provided have increased greatly since World War II. In 1947-48 the historical statistics for funding higher education had totaled $2,037,770,000. By the 1970s revenues for higher education will have exceeded $20 billion.[57]

In 1960-61 some 395,198 bachelor's and first professional degrees were earned, 81,735 master's degrees were earned and 10,575 doctoral degrees (except first professional) were earned. In 1970-71 the corresponding numbers of degrees earned were: 863,000; 224,000 and 32,000. Projections to 1980-81 indicate 1,333,000 bachelor's degrees will be earned, 396,000 master's degrees will be earned, and 68,700 doctoral degrees will be earned.[58]

By 1971-72 the total number of colleges and universities had increased to 2,626. Of this total 1,474 are private and 1,152 are public, but public institutions are growing at a much more rapid rate.[59] The enrollment shift to public educational institutions has been reinforced by the greater proportion of federal funding going to public than to private institutions. In 1966-67 public institutions for the first time received 52 percent of the federal grants and contract funds.[60] Also by 1966 the increases in higher educational physical plants were found to be largely in publically controlled institutions of higher learning.[61]

In sum, it is clear that two things are happening—the educational opportunities for training idea people are increasing dramatically, and secondly, they are being shifted increasingly to public institutions of higher education. These develop-ments make the implementation of a federal manpower policy more feasible because an increasing majority of manpower production is being supplied by governmental agencies. In light of this trend and in the great number of specialists being produced, a manpower policy could be seen as a next logical step.

W hat idea people do is produce knowledge and apply it. In recent decades in urbanized society, it has been clear that idea research and related intellectual activities are knowledge producing. In recent decades it has become increasingly apparent that many executives either are themselves idea people or that they heavily rely on idea people in making decisions. In fact in the last quarter of a century in America, a major new role has evolved for idea people in the form of knowledge application through administration.

The current high position of idea people in the United States is part of the historical and evolutionary process which has made science the heart of Western civilization. Both science and idea people are outgrowths of the search for truth and the material values of the Enlightenment. In this context tolerance, originality, skepticism and pluralism are important societal ingredients.[1]

The new roles for idea people reflect a considerable blurring of the traditionally sharp distinctions between intellectuals and administrators. Traditionally intellectuals have been either abrasive critics of administrative power structures or recluses having little concern about the application of their knowledge by society.[2] In the United States there continue to be traditional intellectuals who largely remove themselves from deci-

5

knowledge production and application

sion-making power and other intellectuals who are sharp critics of power structures. But there are now increasing numbers of actioned-oriented intellectuals, most of whom we have referred to as idea people in this book. The trade-off between this group of intellectuals and administrators has become quite common. The movement of Dean Rusk from university teaching to the State Department back to university teaching, the movement of Senator Humphrey between colleges and the Senate, and the movement of John F. Collins, former mayor of Boston, to MIT all illustrate the increasing variety of roles that intellectuals fill.

In spite of expanded and new roles for idea people, it must still be pointed out that they feel society rewards them less than it should.[3] Nevertheless from the 1940s to the present, studies like those by the National Opinion Research Center reveal that Americans generally hold scientists, in particular, and creative thinkers in general, in high regard. Professors, symphony orchestra musicians, physicians, and top political leaders are all given high ranks. But America's more traditional intellectuals still compare themselves with their European counterparts. In accordance with this comparison they view their prestige in America as lower than that of their European counterparts. A major difference is that many American intellectuals have less direct contact with major political administrators than do their European counterparts. This is partly a result of the larger number of idea people in American society.

Idea people have only come to prominence in the last three decades. One of the most renowned idea persons, James Conant, led the way to new and expanded roles for idea people. During his tenure as president of Harvard University, he supported a significant body of research which, among many important findings, led to the development of the atomic bomb. In the fifties he left Harvard to serve the govern-ment in Germany, ultimately as ambassador to Bonn. In spite of the magnitude of his professional career, his greatest contribution is a personal one. Throughout his career, he encouraged young intellectuals to enter public life, the result being the contributions of creative thinkers which might otherwise have been lost.[4] American intellectuals have become America's idea people. In recent decades all levels of public officials have sought advice from specialists as part of the decision-making process. America's idea people are building a new world that outstrips even their imagination. Their influence is enormous. Traditional pressure groups may get a few million dollars from congressmen. On the other hand, a single space scientist with The National Aeronautics Space Administration may, by using scientific data, get ten times more dollar support from Congress than traditional pressure groups.[5]

Conant's leadership has made its impact. For example when McGeorge Bundy was special assistant to the president, he stressed the importance of high-quality scientists in top policy-level decision making, where intelligence and imagination have direct creative consequences. At one point, he asserted that scientific, military, and political decision making must be integrated into a single process.[6] Intellectual, dynamic, and innovative idea people will increasingly be both in demand and in power.[7]

research production

Idea people through their research and knowledge constitute a major driving force in the economy of urbanized America. Directly and indirectly their work stimulates the development of new products, new industries, and the new jobs.[8] Indeed from the 1940s to the 1970s, nations that have emphasized the production of new ideas and, more particularly, exploited the application of new ideas to practical societal relevance have been world leaders. In this way, what idea people do is the economic lifeblood of all urbanized societies.

Research findings, by long-standing tradition, are freely disseminated and published internationally. Alexander King estimates that, prior to World War II, upward of 70 percent of the world's significant, fundamental scientific research was generated from laboratories in Germany, Great Britain, Scandinavia, the Netherlands and Switzerland. Following World War II there was a redistribution. The United States and Russia became major producers and users of basic and applied research. Since World War II, the American production of basic research, applied research, and technological development have become increasingly interrelated and in many cases inseparable. A whole new magnitude of importance is thereby established for idea people. Government has become a major patron of research and idea people. The patronage, however, is not altruism. The urbanized society is governmentally and economically dependent on high level and aggressive production of new ideas.

Throughout the world in the latter part of the twentieth century, the production of basic and applied research has accelerated. Still it is estimated that there is a five-to-ten-year time lapse between idea production and the development of economically practical material. In America there has been an increased acceptance and utilization of new ideas.[9] As basic research and innovation become normal activity, specific crucial stages of development are recognizable. The stages include product formulation research, engineering development, market research, manufacturing, and distribution.[10] The stages vary with the subject of research—industrial, military, the arts for example—but the principle is clear.

In urbanized societies there is a substantial amount of support for research having practical objectives. For example, the total national investment in research and development, according to a National Science Foundation study, was $25 billion for 1968. While this is an increase over earlier years, the rate of increase is somewhat smaller; nevertheless, government investment provides major support for research and development.[11] Research funds (excluding development funds) in the past decade in all sections of the national economy totalled approximately $6 billion annually, $2 billion for basic research and the other $4 billion for applied research.[12]

knowledge production and application

Slightly over half of the basic research is being performed in colleges and universities, while more than half of the applied research is being carried out by industry.

In 1963 development activities cost $11 billion dollars. About 84 percent of the development work was conducted by industry, with the remainder being performed in part by colleges and universities, government agencies, and nonprofit organizations. By 1967 the distribution of research and development was 13 percent for basic research, 21 percent for applied research and 66 percent for development.[13] In 1956, 7 percent was allocated to basic research, 22 percent to applied research and 71 percent to development. By 1963 basic research had doubled, applied research stayed virtually the same, and development had been reduced somewhat.

The distribution of the research and development effort is also reflected by the employment distribution of scientists and engineers. Nearly 70 percent are employed in industry, where a similar proportion of the federal funding is allocated. Universities and the federal government each have about 10 percent of the personnel for research and 20 percent for development. But the federal government utilized about twice the funding utilized by the universities for carrying out research and development. Under 5 percent of the personnel and federal funding for research and development goes to other nonprofit institutions.

It must be reiterated that the research and idea production are related to age. Most idea people enter their productive periods in the early years of life with creative production peaking in their late thirties and early forties. The careers of many administrators peak after their middle forties. This age-specific contribution of idea people makes the labor market for them very complex. In the following pages research production is examined in universities, agencies, and industry. This analysis will follow the process from basic research through applied research.

idea production in universities

The university research environment is closely tied to teaching. Some professors devote full time to research; others divide their time between teaching and research with the assistance of full-time or part-time research associates, the latter often being part-time students. In addition to regular on-campus research a number of major universities have tangentially attached research and/or development units. In most cases the primary activities of the staff at these facilities is applied research. There may be also some very advanced-level instruction, often at the dissertation or post-doctoral level. In all of these cases from on-campus part-time research to off-campus, but campus-related, full-time research, there is the characteristic exploration for new knowledge through discussion, discourse and seminars that disseminate as well as produce ideas. In high-quality learning environments, it is often difficult to distinguish between researcher and professor in the idea production sense. In essence great researchers are great learners, and great students, by their questions and discourse, are important stimulators to researchers if not themselves producers of new ideas. When students and faculty, particularly graduate students, participate together in research, their collaboration may develop in such a way so that it is difficult, if not impossible, to discern who is the primary producer.

As a result of the university situation, in which there is intermixing between research and teaching, there is an understatement of the number of idea people and dollars which go to support the production of ideas. This is not to dispute that industry has the largest body of personnel and the greatest dollar investment in research. Moreover, it is not to suggest that even most faculty, much less most students, are mainstream participants in idea production. Most faculty members are disseminators of ideas, and most students are consumers.

A few examples of tangentially attached university research laboratories illustrate their importance. Over the past few years notable examples have been: the Stanford Research and Development Park in Palo Alto, California; the Cornell Aeronautical Laboratory in Buffalo, New York; the Cornell Agricultural Experiment Station at Geneva, New York; and the Institute of Social Research adjacent to the University of Michigan at Ann Arbor.[14]

The growth of research enterprise at universities is important. In recent years expenditures for research and development in natural and social sciences has increased from $400 million to well over $700 million. Over 70 percent of the personnel engaged in this research are directly attached to the universities. Another 16 percent are directly and/or indirectly attached to universities through agricultural experiment stations, and a final 12 percent are supported by federal research contracts. The distribution of funding to support researchers varies as follows: 45 percent supplied directly by universities, 39 percent federally supported through contracts, and 16 percent governmentally supported through agricultural experiment stations.

The university learning environment is most characterized by variability, plurality, and multiplicity. The flexibility of the intellectual environment in universities is poignantly illustrated by the following examples. The work of Jay W. Forrester, professor of Management at Massachusetts Institute of Technology illustrates one type of career development. His most recent book is *World Dynamics*, preceded by related books titled *Urban Dynamics* and *Industrial Dynamics*, which received the Academy of Management Award in 1962. Forrester is a member of the National Academy of Engineers, a fellow of the Institute of Electrical and Electronics Engineers, a member of the American Academy of Arts and Sciences, and he is a director of a corporation.[15] In preparing *Urban Dynamics* he was greatly influenced and stimulated by a former mayor of the city of Boston. His B.S. degree was earned at the University of Nebraska and his M.S. degree is from the Massachusetts Institute of Technology. He has been awarded honorary doctorates from the University of Nebraska and from Boston University. In 1968 he received the Inventer of the Year award from George Washington University and in 1969 the Valdemar Poulsen gold metal from the Danish Academy of Technical Sciences. His creative work ranges from systems analysis in the engineering sciences to the application of systems analysis in urban social problems.

Although we could give a rather long and exhaustive list of creative academics who embody this "think differently" attitude, we will limit ourselves to two more examples—B. F. Skinner, the controversial Harvard psychology professor, and Professor William Burch from Yale. In *Beyond Freedom and Dignity,* Skinner calls for a new technology of behavior which will alter the very nature of man.[16] *Daydreams and Nightmares* is a small book by Yale Professor Burch. Although, like many new works, the book and its author remain rather obscure, these essays on environment are vastly important. And although society is fickle in making some ideas more popular than others, idea power is generated from both the obscure and the popular.[17]

Still another dimension of the academic environment is illustrated by the relationships between professional associations like the American Institute of Architects and university schools of architecture. In the mid-1960s, practicing architects and instructors of architects shared an urgent concern about the need for research in architecture to serve both society and the profession. At an AIA architect-researcher conference held on the campus of the University of Michigan, architects expressed the desire to use existing technology and to develop their own technology and research for their own betterment and for the betterment of mankind.[18] The discussions at this meeting went on to indicate that the profession of architecture needed a dynamic program of research which would be cross-disciplinary, involving both hard and soft sciences. Going beyond design and engineering there was specific concern with sociology, psychology, computer technology, chemistry, space, and medicine. Architects were not seeking to become experts in all of these areas, but they wanted to be sufficiently conversant with them to utilize their findings to

knowledge production and application

develop better living environments. The professors of architecture and the practitioners were concerned with training architect-researchers as well as with the use of research developed by others. The net effect has been a considerable modification in the curriculum of architects which has emphasized a greater capacity for doing research in both academic institutions and the profession.[19]

Virtually all major professions relate in a similar manner to university environments by supporting new directions in university research.

agencies and research

Government agencies, quasi-government agencies, and private or foundation-type research organizations are all included in the following discussion. It is appropriate to differentiate idea production in agencies from that in universities, or in industries only in operational terms. Idea production is not really separated into categories like university, agency, and industry. The basic nature of ideas and the freedom with which researchers pursue their ideas provides for a considerable amount of interaction among researchers in all of these categories. Nevertheless, there is sufficiently different focus in these environments to warrant discussing them as though they were separate to a considerable degree.

It already has been pointed out that researchers in the university environment are most devoted to basic inquiry—unique and different patterns of investigation. Agency people mainly concentrate on applied research. This will be illustrated in the following paragraphs when the types of agencies are enumerated. Agency idea people, by the nature of their mission, however, may engage both in basic and applied research. The proportion of basic and applied research may change from place to place and time to time as the focus of a particular mission is modified.

In industry, researchers disproportionately focus their activities on applied research, but basic "think tanks" are being expanded in certain research areas.

Major types of governmental research agencies include the U.S. Department of Defense, the U.S. Department of Agriculture, National Aeronautics and Space Administration, the U.S. Department of Interior, the U.S. Department of Commerce, the U.S. Department of Health, Education and Welfare, and the Veterans Administration. In addition to these one must add the National Science Foundation which primarily funds other individuals to do research in contrast to the previously listed agencies, which carry out most of their own research by in-house operations. Other independent agencies with considerable mission focus are: the Atomic Energy Commission, the U.S. Weather Bureau, the National Bureau of Standards and its Central Radio Propogation Laboratory, the Coast and Geodetic Survey, the Hydrographic Office, the Geological Survey, the Office of Science and Technical Information, the Antarctic Office of the Navy Department, the Antarctic Program of the National Science Foundation, the Fish and Wildlife Service and the Naval Observatory.[20]

Another important category of what has come to be known as "big science" focuses on basic research that is carried out through special kinds of expensive facilities. These include nuclear particle accelerators, large radio and optical telescopes, oceanographic research vessels, and scientific satellites. In addition, and much related to universities, are institutes like Brookhaven National Laboratory, Kitt Peak Astronomical Observatory and the National Center for Atmospheric Research.[21]

Creative scientific research is presently carried on in most areas, including physics, chemistry, other physical sciences, mathematics and statistics, biological sciences, social sciences, (including economics), foreign agriculture affairs, history and anthropology, geography and cartography, psychology, and operations research. In addition idea people work in the major professional areas of engineering and health. Nearly half of all the nonprofessional idea personnel are associated with engineering, another almost 20 percent are in mechanics, and approximately 15 percent are in the biological sciences. The other nontechnical idea personnel range widely.

Much, if not most, of what idea people do in agency work is related to security and national defense. Prior to World War II a great deal of the basic research used in America was produced in Europe. Idea people in the United States took the basic idea and, through the mechanisms of applied research, gave dynamic thrust for material and social developments. During and following World War II the U.S. encouraged activity in basic research and developed the capacity to produce most of its own basic as well as applied research. Since then, both science and engineering became so important to national affairs that agencies such as the Atomic Energy Commission, the National Science Foundation, the National Aeronautics and Space Administration and the Department of Health, Education and Welfare were established. Other initiatives include the creation of the position of Special Assistant to the President for Science and Technology, the Federal Council for Science and Technology, and the President's Science Advisory Committee. In addition to these new agencies, posts and advisory committees there was a major exapnsion in research and development on the part of the Department of Defense.[22]

With this massive expansion of agencies and quasi agencies, the roles and functions of managing research production have become an increasing matter of concern and debate. For some there is a growing fear that technocrats will constitute an elite or become a major power structure in government. From the governmental point of view and on a more pragmatic level, there is a need to plan more systematically for the support of the various types of research. Accordingly there have been numerous proposals for the organization of what might be called a Department of Science and Technology at the cabinet level in the federal government. Prestigious scientists and advisory groups have either not spoken in favor of such a department or have been openly against it. The fact that bills have been introduced into the Congress in recent years for the establishment of a science-oriented department is in itself a significant index of the importance of idea people in American society. Arguments for a department of science and technology includes issues like operational effectiveness and organizational efficiency. The continuity, expansion and/or retrenchment in the production of new research needs increasingly to be systematically planned in order to utilize fully their abilities and capacities.

Research production is costly in terms of time, lives, and dollars. Congress is continually pressed to be more efficient in funding scientists and engineers and to be more systematic in setting priorities for their work. The question of more and higher status for idea people also continues. Some who propose a national department of science submit that the creation of such a department would bring higher status to idea people. Others argue for a federal department of science on the basis that such a department would insure that appropriate areas for research are supported through centralized planning rather than left to chance and the influences of pressure groups. Or, put another way, when left to their own designs, researchers tend to specialize and focus intensely on increasingly narrow issues, often overspecializing and failing to see the "big picture." A government agency working in this area would presumably have as one of its responsibilities the development of an overview of the big picture for science and engineering. It would identify gaps and areas in which more research is needed. Such an agency would help in the channeling of personnel and funds to priority areas.[23]

The range of applied research in agencies is enormous. In most cases the agency name is sufficient to illustrate the content of much of the work, for example: the Department of Health, Education and Welfare, which supports research in the three respective areas: the Department of Agriculture, concerned with research in the food and fiber industry; the Department of Defense, responsible for research concerning military hardware; the Department of the Interior, with research concerning natural resources; and many others. There are, in addition, numerous types of obscure applied research projects in these agencies. The Department of Agriculture, through its Forest Service, and the Department of Commerce's National Park Service both support research on people. Their subjects concern, for example, what people like and dislike about camping in the National Parks, why there are man-caused forest fires, what are the life styles among migrant farm workers and the rural poor in general, and so forth. In the U.S. Department of Labor there are numerous research projects that concern policy related, for example, to the propriety of using tax funds for up-graded training and the impact of supporting migration of workers from one region of the nation to another, in addition to the routine research that concerns labor market trends and projections.

One of the most poignant examples of the controversial research conducted in some applied agencies is illustrated by the U.S. Army's sponsorship of Project Camelot in the mid-1960s. The army, in supporting this research, had intended to be able to measure and forecast the causes of revolution and insurgency in underdeveloped areas. From the point of view of most researchers involved in the project, this was basic social science research to be carried out over a four-year period and costing from $4 to $6 million. The areas for the research were to include Latin America, Asia, Africa and Europe. The U.S. Army funded this research project through the Special Operations Research Organization, which had a tangential relationship to the American University in Washington, D.C. In addition to initial work in Chile, it was recommended that the project cover: Argentina, Bolivia, Brazil, Columbia, Cuba, Dominican Republic, El Salvador, Guatemala, Mexico, Paraguay, Peru and Venezuela (in Latin America); Egypt, Iran, and Turkey (in the Middle East); Korea, Indonesia, Malaysia, and Thailand, (the Far East); and France, Greece and Nigeria.

Although the work for Project Camelot was not classified

and theoretically, therefore, there was no stigma of secrecy, much criticism soon originated in Chile and from the U.S. State Department. Shortly afterward the project was terminated by the secretary of defense. The prospect or fate of such a project is not the subject of issue here; however, it serves as an example of the controversial areas that idea people have been involved in.[24]

Similarly controversial research is carried on in other areas, including: national data banks and the associated concerns for invasion of individual privacy; concerning sterilization, artificial insemination, and birth control; and weather modification.

The arts are also supported by a variety of agencies. In 1965 the federal government passed the Arts and Humanities Bill. With this congressional action the National Foundation on the Arts and Humanities was established. The initial appropriation was some $63 million. It supports idea people in the following ways: awards for excellence to painters and sculptors; art resources surveys; aid to museums; commissions which provide experimental work in areas like silk screening and lithographs; experimentation in theatre; research for the scientific study of new art materials; research concerning the relation of art and artists to law; sabbatical leaves for novelists, poets, painters, sculptors, composers and so forth; and travel grants.[25] In spite of the broad range of support for artists, there is fear that this type of agency support for the arts may mean government control of artistic research and production. While this is not officially the intent nor is it hardly probable, it does reflect the fierceness with which idea people guard their independence and the magnitude of official support for creative people.

idea people in industry

Research people in industry have strong orientations toward applied problems. In the last two decades their activities and the importance of their work have increased sharply. The number of dollars allocated to industrial research and the number of persons employed have increased precipitously. Shortly after the turn of the century $3.6 billion were allocated for industrial research and development; the figure has increased more than three times that amount.

The overwhelming majority, approximately three-fourths, of the nation's research and development work is done in private industry, and the largest proportion of the private industry's work is in fact funded by the federal government.[26] The remainder of the federal government's research and development is carried out in its own laboratories, by universities, and by other nonprofit organizations. A great amount of industrial research is in the area of aircraft, missiles, and space exploration. Major private industry research areas include: optical, surgical, photographic, and other instruments (83 percent increase between 1956 and 1960); food and related products (83 percent increase); drugs and medicines (79 percent increase); machinery (77 percent increase); and primary metals (76 percent increase). The highest increase was for scientific and mechanical measuring instruments (135 percent). Motor vehicle and other transportation showed the lowest percent increase (27 percent). From 1956 to 1960, funds for research and development in all types of industry increased by 61 percent.[27]

In addition to federal funding to private industry for research and development, company-sponsored research and development is increasing. In 1960 the dollar value for industry-supported research was $4.4 billion compared to $2.2 billion in 1953. Personnel, like dollar value, for industrial research and development are increasing substantially. By the mid-1960s there were approximately 348,700 research and development scientists and engineers in full-time employment in American industries.[28] There are increases in research personnel throughout industry, the largest proportion of researchers being in aircraft-and missile-related jobs, the next largest proportion in electrical equipment and communications, followed by high proportions in chemical, machinery, and transportation jobs. The remaining small proportion are employed in a wide range of jobs. It must be remembered that most research and development people work in private industry as private employees on projects that are most often funded by the federal government. Their research is primarily for national defense and for social welfare.

A closer examination of the "new look" in American industry is essential to understand what idea people do there. In this last part of the twentieth century, industry is in a new environment and a new fight for survival. The shift is to more accurate and systematic data for decision making and away from reliance on the charismatic, "captain-of-industry" unilateral decision-making approach.[29] The educational level of corporate employees is increasing, and creativity and innovation are being rewarded more in industry. Indeed, staff-type organization is increasingly being used in contemporary corporation. More specialists than ever before are being employed on staffs to render professional information and judgments as corporations attempt to compete in an ever more complex technological society. There is increasing effort to change the image of the corporation from a rigid autocratic structure to an energy exchange system. In this case creative energy from new ideas is focused on new goals and transformed as it goes through the corporation to provide a product. The "Man in the Gray Flannel Suit," and the "corporation takeover," are on the way out; the creative organization with personnel participation is on the way in. The new corporation is, therefore, heavily staffed with idea people, who, besides being professionals, are often more "cosmopolitans" than "locals." This is to say they are more loyal to their profession in engineering, law, science, or whatever than to their employer.

Idea people are also employed to participate in defining and creating the functional roles and goals of corporations. In effect new management decision making is increasingly a matter of creativity, and the new organizational chart for corporations has two levels rather than one (see Figure 5.1).

knowledge production and application

figure 5.1
two level organizational chart—solid lines connecting offices and dotted lines connecting idea people

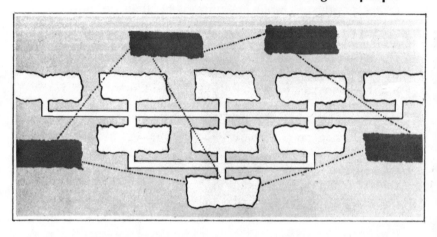

Source: "The Corporation as a Creative Environment," *Kaiser News* 1 (1973), 20.

The one level represents the more traditional line organization from the board of directors to the president, to the vice-presidents, through the various department heads, and so forth. The second level connects a series of specialists including engineers, lawyers, scientists, technological experts, writers, designers, analysts, and many others. They work with each other and relate to top management in the corporation.

By the mid-1970s it is expected that approximately two hundred of the nation's largest corporations will control approximately 75 percent of the nation's output of materials and ideas.[30] Increasingly therefore, the large corporations provide for their own internal use both basic and applied research laboratories. The following examples indicate the impact of corporations and researchers on basic and applied research:

1. *Air conditioning:* At the end of the nineteenth century, air moisturizing was invented for use in cotton mills. By 1906 air cooling was invented, and by 1970 some 35 percent of American homes were cooled by twenty-three million air conditioners.

2. *Automobiles:* The first gas-operated car was driven in America in 1892. Three years later there were still only four cars, but in 1900 there were eighty automobile firms, including Henry Ford's. Nearly one-thousand cars were manufactured that year. Shortly Ford developed the Model-T and mass-produced it. By 1927 it was bought by fifteen million people. By 1970 the automobile industry had an investment totaling $1.47 billion and a payroll of nearly nine hundred thousand people. By 1970 some ninety-two million cars, representing an investment of $46 billion, were owned in the United States.

3. *Telephones:* In the 1870s telephones were first introduced in America. By 1900 there were a million subscribers. In 1970 telephones in America carried over five hundred million calls a day. Telephone investments totaled more than $75 billion, and nearly a million persons were employed.

4. *Television:* The origins of television are as early as the 1880s with the disc scanner. The photo tube was invented in 1914, the iconoscope in 1923, and by 1939 television was a reality. Following World War II it was used by nearly 100 percent of American households, slightly over half with color. Annual manufacture of radio and TV sets passed the $4.5 billion level in 1970. Over 150,000 employees work in the television industry.

5. *Cameras:* This invention precedes industrial America. "Camera obscura" originated in sixteenth-century Italy. In the 1880s Eastman improved the camera. By 1970 there were over five hundred camera manufacturers employing some 114,000 workers. They produce over $3 billion worth of photo equipment.

6. *Washing machines:* The ancestor to the modern laundry machine dates from the 1850s. By the 1930s the annual production was more than one million, and by 1970 over 90

percent of all households were equipped with home laundries. Annual sales exceed $50 million.

7. *Electric lights:* Edison introduced the electric light in 1878. The success of electric lighting spread rapidly. By the 1970s more than $6 billion worth of lighting equipment was produced annually. Employees in this industry total more than two hundred thousand.[31]

The rapid development of these inventions was made possible by the close collaboration of industry, government, and the universities. While the universities remained the main creative centers for researchers, government and industry made possible the implementation and popular utilization of new products.

In the 1950s and early 1960s bright young specialists tended to turn from industry to seek work in universities and government where they could fulfill more completely their desires to serve society. With the major changes in the posture of industry since the mid-1960s it has been increasingly effective in attracting bright young idea people.[32] Many researchers desire work in environments where they can see their ideas refined and used; industry is a prime location for such persons. Also the increased emphasis on basic research in industry has drawn idea people from liberal arts as well as business backgrounds. While industry wants problem solving, it also wants creative answers. Research in industry is increasingly directed toward the production as well as the implementation of new ideas.[33]

The new industrial use of idea people is further illustrated by the case of the Ford Motor Company in the employment of two hundred young Ph.D.'s many of whom have often been referred to as the "Whiz Kids at Ford."[34] At Ford these idea people engage in a considerable amount of basic research and applied research. What they do is illustrated by Allen Turner's new process of curing paint in a matter of seconds by electronic radiation and avoiding the longer heat process. The new process is useful on wood, plastic, and metal. Out of much basic research this is one of the many products being tested for practical application.

Some industrial research laboratories have emerged with illustrious distinction—indeed competing with universities in the area of basic research. Among them, one continually finds the General Electric and Bell Telephone Laboratories and, with almost equal frequency, Kodak, International Business Machines, Shell Development, DuPont, Union Carbide, Dow, and Monsanto.[35] In industry the amount of time allocated to scientists for basic research tends to vary from about 5 to 25 percent. This is usually referred to as time for "going fishing." In fact research directors find that the problem with basic research in industry is keeping the researchers working on basic subjects: they become so intrigued by the ways in which their fundamental research can be applied that they tend to go off the fundamental and long-range and into applied.[36] Industrial interest in basic research continues to magnify because the time lag between basic discovery and application is being sharply reduced; the feedback in applied research has considerable economic value, and this enables the basic researchers to avoid the faddism often found in university research.[37]

Even in smaller industrial firms, the function of research is expanding to include technical intelligence, pilot operations and technical service as well as the more traditional areas of quality control, maintenance and repair, process improvement, estimating and evaluation, etc.[38] While it is difficult for small and medium-sized firms to support substantial research laboratories, their ability to compete is increasingly restricted without new ideas. Therefore, research is being expanded in all industrial levels.

geographical distribution of research

In recent years research and development funds totaled $13 billion. Thirty-four percent of this expenditure was in the western region and another thirty percent in the Northeast.

At the state level California ranked first with 27 percent of the total, New York ranked second, and New Jersey third. In other words, the three states of California, New York and New Jersey together accounted for more than one-half of the total national research and development expenditures. The Far West received the greatest proportion of federal support for research and development. More than half of research and development in the East is funded by private industry. The distribution of federal funding for research and development in private industry significantly favors the West.

administrative application of knowledge

A second major role for idea people is administration. Through the rest of the twentieth century and probably well into the twenty-first century, administrators will need to be well-versed idea people and not simply mechanical users of ideas. Conant, in the middle of the twentieth century, wrote that " . . . in order to assimilate science into the culture of our 20th Century highly industrialized society, we must regard scientific theories as guides to human action and thus an extension of common sense."[39] In other words administration must take regular cognizance of and make regular use of scientific knowledge.

This new and important role for idea people is clearly illustrated by McGeorge Bundy when he said that he was not really an intellectual, but a recognizer of and user of ideas in his administration.[40] Indeed, one of the marks of modern administrators is the recognition and use of creativity in others. The orderly uses and application of knowledge are difficult and challenging. Evaluating the durability of new ideas is difficult. In our rapidly changing technological society ideas have often been applied before they have been sufficiently tested. The results of premature application of processes is costly, and faulty products erode industrial profit making. This kind of expensive mistake, along with an unwillingness on the part of executives to take risks, is sufficient to retire many administrators at an early age.

Contemporary administrators have two roles: authority manifestation and power exercise. Both are important and precarious. Minor administrators may be rapidly elevated to top positions as others, with equal speed, fall to obscurity. Systematic information in-put to creative decision making rather than charisma is the essence of the modern exercise of power.

authority manifestation

Many of today's idea people sit in top councils where research findings are used to mold major policy on critical issues. However, they generally present information, while the final use of the information is left to administrators. This specialized in-put from the new "think tanks" or "think factories" constitutes a difficult adjustment for many executives and administrators.[41] The case is illustrated by the example of a group of Harvard and MIT professors in the mid-1950s. They began meeting regularly, once a week, to discuss the application of knowledge to societal problems. Their immediate concern was the nearness of nuclear destruction of the world. By 1960 these professors saw their concerns expressed in speeches of the then presidential candidate John Kennedy. Within another year several of them, Jerome Weisner, McGeorge Bundy, Arthur Schlesinger, Jr., and Carl Kaysen, held White House posts. From their new administrative posts they saw their ideas put into laws like the test-ban treaty.[42]

The influence that specialists have on administrators is complex and often controversial. These complexities and controversies are illustrated in the case of the so-called Moynihan Report, *The Negro Family: The Case for National Action.*[43] The conclusions of the report were the results of the application of social science findings to governmental use. On the other hand, it has been argued that the report is in fact neither basic research nor a technical document but, rather, a

knowledge production and application

polemic.[44] By any standard, administrative action in the area of Negro or black employment and Negro or black family assistance is "sensitive" if not controversial. Social science scholars differ on some of the details in the Moynihan Report, but to many it seemed very much in line with other standard interpretations.

In this book we are not concerned with the validity or lack of validity of Moynihan's interpretation or even technically with his subject matter. We are concerned with the principle and processes of interacting idea authority with administration. Therefore, it is necessary to note that Mr. Moynihan joined the government in 1961 as part of the New Frontier. Initially he was a special assistant to Secretary of Labor Goldberg. By 1963 he had been elevated to the post of assistant secretary of labor in charge of the Office of Policy, Planning and Research. His professional credentials are sterling. He attended the City College of New York and Tufts University. He earned a Ph.D. in Political Science at the Fletcher School of Law and Diplomacy, and he attended the London School of Economics on a Fulbright Fellowship. With this intellectual background, he entered public service and became one of the new scientist-politicos. He had for some time been an integral part of the government, so much so that the report was prepared as "a member of the Presidential Government who has the right to suggest policy of a sweeping nature. . . ."[45]

Moynihan was acquainted with the "careful style" government report and with the more decisive risk-taking report. He opted for the latter strategy fully cognizant of its potential consequences. Indeed his strategy is one which suggests that careful data gathering and analysis are important but insufficient and that idea people ought to assume administrative authority and responsibility for seeing their data and analysis incorporated into policy. By the nature of the structure of administrative hierarchies, tension exists between line members in the organization and staff specialists. Moynihan's effort was to use the authority of his training and office to override the traditional chain of command and put social science data directly into policy-making positions.[46]

Regardless of the facts of the situation, the Moynihan Report was "leaked" beyond the secretary of labor directly to staff in the president's office. Some of the report was incorporated into a presidential speech. A White House conference dealing with Negro family life was set. Action resulted at, and beyond, the policy level, and it had gone with lightning speed beyond the regular channels. Whether proper authority had or had not been exercised in preparing the report, it was the type of subject matter that could be attacked on "intellectual" grounds. Both political and intellectual attacks followed, precipitating a nearly explosive controversy which ultimately led to Mr. Moynihan's termination as assistant secretary of labor.

Cases of this type illustrate the need for balancing the authority of specialists and intellectuals with that of politicians. Regardless of the factual correctness of specialists' recommendations, they do not survive on authority alone. They must have administrative support for survival.

There are various advisory-type councils in government administrative circles that are staffed by specialists who have more than ordinary opportunity to manifest authority in the creative building of policy. The establishment of a Council of Economic Advisors in 1946 is one case in point.[47] This advisory group was established by congressional action as a statutory agency in the office of the president. The members of this advisory council are by the nature of its position idea people. Their job is to coordinate technical expertise and to utilize it in developing policy, to contribute to the drafting of legislation, and to participate in evaluating a whole range of economic issues faced by the nation. In this case idea authority, as specified by Congress, has direct routes of in-put into the decision-making system. In some cases the Council of Economic Advisors is required to make specific recommendations to the government.

Another important advisory agency is the National Security Council, which was created by the National Security Act of 1947. Two years later it too became a part of the executive office. This is a statutory policy-making body with a specified membership including: the president, the vice-president, the secretary of state, the secretary of defense, the director of the Office of Defense Mobilization and the director of Foreign Operations Administration. Other individuals may be invited to attend the National Security Council meetings at the pleasure of the president. This council is specifically charged and given responsibility for advising the president on the integration of domestic, foreign and military policies as they relate to the nation's security.

The National Security Council, unlike the Council of Economic Advisors, has administrative functions, but by its structure its members are not expected to have a common area of expertise. In subsequent years many additional advisory bodies have been established to receive advice from experts concerning the various operations of American society.[48]

University faculty consultants since World War II have constituted a major source of talent for government both in research and in administration. Their employment has included work for private industry, private and quasi-private agencies, and for local, state, national, and international governments. This pattern of activity has become so prevalent in universities that consulting policies have been established to deal with conflicts of interest, interference with university functions, and other ethical matters.[49]

In 1963 the National Science Foundation surveyed fifty-nine universities whose faculties do three-fourths of the research and development work used in consulting for the government. Table 5.1 summarizes the findings. Fifty-four universities responded to the study, and all of them permit their faculty to participate in consulting work. Forty-seven of these universities have a formal policy concerning consulting work. The major policy questions are: requirement of prior approval, limitations on time spent, limitations on money earned, use of university space and equipment, employment of students and reduction of teaching loads, and leaves of absence. In most cases limitations on time spent and prior approvals are required. There are few limitations on use of space and equipment, and employment of students is generally not controlled.

table 5.1

consulting policies and practices of selected colleges and universities

idea	number responding to specific questions [a]	
	yes	no
total permitting consulting	54	0
institutions with formal policy on consulting	47	7
policy:		
required prior approval	36	18[b]
limited time spent	39	15
limited money earned	2	50
permitted use of space	21	33
permitted use of equipment	18	36
permitted employment of graduate students	20	31
permitted reduction of teaching loads	6	48
permitted leave of absence	28	26
limited type of consulting	32	21
limited organizations for which consulting could be undertaken	8	46
required reports of—		
time spent	22	31
fees earned	5	48

Source: "Faculty Consulting," *Reviews of Data on Science Resources,* NSF, No. 8, (February, 1968), 2.

[a] Institutions did not respond to all questions. Therefore "yes" and "no" totals do not necessarily add to 54.

[b] Seven of these institutions did require notification from a faculty member before he undertook consulting.

knowledge production and application

It was found that universities feel that consulting furnishes considerable potential advantage for adding to a faculty member's individual experience, for increasing the body of knowledge, and for enhancing the prestige of the school. Indeed it is viewed as part of an appropriate public service role. Negative concerns relate to conflicts of interest and related to the erosion of time faculty can spend with resident students.

One special form of authority manifestation is shown by the expert witness. Especially in cases involving complex social and legal problems, expert witnesses are increasingly called; often they are research professionals in private industry, universities or other agencies. Reliance on the opinions of specialists has grown to the point that their expertise in a specified body of knowledge is systematically being sought in administering legal questions of justice in the society.[50] Experts are also called to testify at congressional hearings and at public hearings on special subjects. In such cases their authoritative information becomes a direct part of administrative decision making.

The authority that idea people command can be seen by the number of professional associations that advise government groups and provide constructive outlets for professional disagreement. One example is the American Institute of Architects, who advise the General Service Administration on the design of federal buildings to be constructed throughout the nation. Most federal buildings are designed by registered architects in the state where the buildings are located. In addition an advisory panel of architects establish the criteria by which local architects are selected, review General Services Administration design standards, advise the administration on the selection of architects and, finally, advise on the acceptability of designs.[51] Design professionals have prepared a statement of principles indicating appropriate criteria for professional selection. The statement is subscribed to by the American Institute of Architects, the American Institute of Consulting Engineers, the American Institute of Planners, the American Society of Civil Engineers, the American Society of Landscape Architects, the Consulting Engineers Council of the United States, and the National Society of Professional Engineers.[52] This document details the selection of prime professionals, the coordination of their work, contractual responsibilities, rates and conditions of compensation, and related matters.

Idea people often manifest their authority by dissent. In an open society, freedom of expression is part of the way of life. This is nowhere more strongly expressed than among creative people in administrative or research roles. It is their nature to "think differently." Authoritarianism is foreign both to creative people and to the mood of democratic societies; conversely, freedom of expression can stimulate higher quality thinking and a higher quality environment. Conformity that stifles new idea production is counterproductive. On the other hand, dissension can threaten the basic equilibrium necessary for social stability and creative throught, and excessive dissidence can also be counterproductive and destroy the stability necessary for a creative working environment.

The situation was clearly illustrated in the bitter conflict between the University of California faculty and the board of regents and the governor of the state.[53] Early in 1949 it appeared that members of the board of regents and the university president, not minor idea people themselves, were favorably disposed to a loyalty oath.[54] The president had not sufficiently consulted his academic advisors, and the faculty—in predictable form—thought differently. With the initial request for accepting an oath, none accepted at La Jolla, 40 percent at Los Angeles, 50 percent at Berkeley, contrasted with 100 percent at Mt. Hamilton and Riverside (at that time Riverside was primarily an agricultural experiment station).[55] Controversy became rampant and questions of morale and academic freedom were raised vehemently. It was pointed out by some that oath requirements would be readily accepted in fact and utterly nonbinding in behavior for many idea people. For others the principle of requiring a loyalty oath was unacceptable in fact even when they were prepared to be loyal in their professional behavior. The result of this confrontation was that everyone—faculty, students, the university administration, and the general public—suffered.

There have been a number of instances in which creative people have used the authority of their positions to influence administrative policies. Scientists and engineers—both faculty and students—at the Massachusetts Institute of Technology and a number of other major universities planned and carried out a "research strike" on March 4, 1969.[56] The concern of the organizers and participants in this research strike was the misuse of scientific and technical knowledge so that it actually threatened the existence of mankind. Biologists, chemists, and physicists were particularly concerned with the overemphasis on building destructive military materials. By bringing all research to a halt for one day they planned to dramatize their concern. In addition to striking, the participants carried out seminars, lectures, and planned discussions in what they viewed as positive new directions. They sought to devise means for turning research application away from overemphasis on military technology toward the solution of environment and social problems. The intent was to impress upon students the vision and hope that the benefits of science and technology have for mankind. Researchers were encouraged to question and study the issues before participating in the designing of destructive weapon systems.[57]

The March fourth strike extended from coast to coast in major programs at MIT, Stanford University, Cornell, Rockefeller University, Columbia, Yale, Carnegie-Mellon, Rutgers, Northwestern, Maryland, University of Colorado, and the University of California at Berkeley and at Irvine, to name only a few. The day was characterized by voluntary dissent without force or violence. It opened discussion and gave impetus to a new direction that has continued to question vested interests.

Dissent and protest have also been expressed by idea people in the arts. In recent years a considerable amount of social criticism is found at theatre performances, in poetry, novels, and the visual arts. Many artists have sought to touch the social conscience of the viewer or reader by putting men's daily and often small actions in a meaningful broad perspective. They help with poignant expression to belittle the ridiculous, to enlarge the grand, and ennoble humanitarian concerns.

Visual artists, painters and sculptors, in the Los Angeles area in the mid-1960s felt that they could no longer work in peace in an environment so rent by conflict and war. They said, "We artists today, each day attempt to summon creative energy in an atmosphere polluted with the crime, the moral decay that is the reality of the war in Viet Nam. It is no longer possible to work in peace."[58] Accordingly these artists called on their colleagues throughout the United States and around the world to organize an exhibition expressing their concern through their artistic medium. Vacant land near a busy intersection in Los Angeles was rented for the exhibition. Entries came from Los Angeles, New York, Paris, Rome, and other cultural centers. The focal point was a sixty-five-foot structure symbolizing the concern of artists the world over. Some of the entries directly expressed the cruelty and inhumanity of social conflict in general while others expressed frustration and opposition to war.

Like striking scientists and engineers, the artists attempt to say in visual form what is wrong and unacceptable and, in juxtaposition, to express the vision of the possibility of a better human environment.

Literary artists protesting the violence in contemporary society have used overt forms of protest. For example, poets, writers and actors have held "read-ins for peace in Viet Nam."[59] They have sent telegrams and petitions and staged marches to and before the White House all expressing dissent concerning military violence. At a National Book Award ceremony, editors and writers walked out on the vice president of the United States to express their opposition. At other times they have put on week-long protest festivals. Film technicians, architects, and artists have joined in week-long discussions

knowledge production and application

precipitating expressions and resolutions against America's Vietnam involvement. The list of artistic expressions for a more human society is a long one. They have sought first to challenge administrators positively and, when all else fails, to frustrate them negatively. Literary artists have responded to specific events in a similar manner. In memorial volumes after the assassination of John F. Kennedy, they called for dignity in the arts as a sign for serious civilization and for health in the political state. A volume edited by Erwin A. Glikes and Paul Schwaber titled *Of Poetry and Power* is one example of such expression.[60]

It is clear that idea people, as we have used the term, do not simply produce research; they are greatly concerned about the application of the knowledge they produce. They express their concern to those in authority through consultation and, when necessary, through dissent.

the exercise of power

The final phase in the new role that researchers fill is participation in the exercise of power. World War II was the stimulus for moving research and development into the mainstream of society. Following the war, idea people have been called upon, and feel required, to follow their ideas into use. White argues that in the decade of the 1960s action-oriented intellectuals have become a new force in American life. They are the most provocative and compelling influence on society.[61]

Ideas are sought everywhere in contemporary American society They are mercilessly and quickly tested against reality—in all levels of government, industry, unions, university administrations, and in other places. The influx of new ideas into society is so great that the norms of science are coming to be regarded as extensions of common sense and appropriate, if not required, guides to human action.[62] But while societal norms provide for broad scientific utilization in decision making, the interaction between the exercise of power and the production of scientific ideas is marvelously complex.[63] Powerful people are users of science, and they also directly and indirectly influence the direction of science. For example, in the National Science Foundation alone, the budget for 1971 allocated $34 million to "Research Applied to National Needs." In 1972 an estimated $56 million will be spent in this category, and by 1973 it is estimated that some $80 million will be allocated for this kind of research. In juxtaposition, during the same three-year period, National Science Foundation funds for science graduate student support will have decreased from $30.5 million to $20 million to $14 million.[64] Even in an agency primarily devoted to basic research, the exercise of power by administrators is used to influence the amount of support for idea people in priority areas.

Specialists and experts have become more and more important sources of information for administrative decision making. Executives who lack accurate technical information will find it difficult to launch and control new programs, and they will lack the necessary intelligence to expand existing programs. Since the 1950s there has been a steady increase in the number of books devoted to intelligence-gathering techniques. Two examples are: Harry Howe Ransom, *Central Intelligence and National Security* (Cambridge: Harvard University Press, 1958) and Washington Platt, *Strategic Intelligence Production: Basic Principles* (New York: Frederick A. Praeger, Inc., 1957). Intelligence-gathering techniques are also disseminated through conferences and symposiums.

No less an office than the presidency of the United States illustrates the exercise of power by an idea person and with the assistance of idea people. How the president of a nation or any similar major administrator is a creative executive and how he uses power is a subject of many studies.[65] The president's job is to search for ideas and information and then to search for people who can be influenced to carry out the decisions once made. It is reported that when Franklin Roosevelt was president he often covertly or even overtly pitted his advisors in competition as he searched for ideas and information. Presidents Truman and Eisenhower, from different backgrounds and traditions, both relied heavily on their staffs for generating ideas. Truman, however, left himself purposely open and accessible for ideas from other sources. Eisenhower remained carefully and studiously more within the lines of the organizational chart. Kennedy expanded his sources of information to include the regular use of study groups for special urgent problems. Johnson expanded this approach to include the task-force operation. While on the one hand it may be argued that the presidency is increasingly becoming the position of a high-powered clerk, it is also clear that presidents are aggressively seeking and expanding their sources of ideas beyond mere clerkmanship. In the case of presidents or governors, the chief administrator is offered two sources of power: creative executive decision making by using expert advice and the use of the veto in the legislative process. A creative administrator may participate legislatively by defending or sustaining an idea ultimately with the veto—a role far more important than a clerk's.

The cabinet is the traditional institution used by chief administrators to seek ideas and reaction to their own ideas before promulgating executive decisions. Cabinet-level officers often constitute an array of idea people—experts and specialists in a number of areas participating in high-level decision making.[66] Numerous cabinet officers have previously been idea businessmen or idea university professors.[67] The cabinet, in effect, may be a presidential advisory board which, if used fully and does its job well, reduces a top executive's margin of ignorance and appreciably expands his level of information. To a great extent the usefulness of the cabinet is influenced by the character of the president because he undoubtedly will influence the direction of its work; for example, an agenda may be established in advance, but the president's opening of a cabinet meeting with observations of his own immediate concern and subjects he considers important may direct the discussion and significantly influence the information and data generated. Indeed cabinet meetings

idea people

may vary considerably from data gathering to data reporting or focus on the formulation of policy—indeed even the establishment of policy.

It has long been known, and perhaps has even become traditional, that there is a hierarchical ranking among the cabinet members. This is referred to as the "inner cabinet," or the "kitchen cabinet."[68] This discriminating use of cabinet members may reflect the subject areas in which critical decisions must be made, or it may even reflect judgments concerning the quality of the information rendered. In any event while the cabinet may be used in a variety of ways, it presently is but one of the several types of advisory bodies and sources of information available to a creative executive.

Certainly, in effect, at the top level of executive power, the administrator is challenged to seek broad ranges of information and to integrate them into effective policy. Some suggest that we are moving toward a new cybernocracy": in the White House there sits a computer optimizing the political well-being of individuals. In a cybernocracy ideas would be contributed by all citizens and would be voted on by all citizens to establish the most popularly desired environmental conditions.[69]

Union leadership illustrates another major area in which the exercise of power is increasingly a matter of information.[70] For many years, elitist groups in America have been challenged, if not frustrated, by abrasive labor leaders expounding alternative ideas and ideologies. More recently traditional elitist groups are challenged by intellectuals on all fronts as the plurality of the culture and the significance of systematic ideas erode charisma, individualism and authoritarianism. Labor union leaders in America have traditionally been at best renegade idea people, and more often they have fit the stereotype as users of abrasive force rather than of idea people. In fact, union leaders have often played the role of creative thinkers. Nevertheless they are most characteristically viewed as outside of or a threat to vested interests. Indeed there has been a general reluctance to recognize ideas by persons other than the intelligentsia.

knowledge production and application

By the 1930s the circumstances for the exercise of power by labor union leaders changed. While the national spirit of rugged individualism persisted, the Great Depression of the 1930s altered it significantly. Moreover another advantage developed for unions: many professionally educated college young people during the depression years were unable to obtain jobs in careers related to their training, so they joined union-related employment as a matter of last resort. Thus, high-powered intellects came into the service of labor unions. Some of these young intellectuals became imbued with union philosophy and have continued to the present day to give labor leaders data, analysis and expertise similar to that available to management. Accordingly, while the style of labor leaders continues to be overtly aggressive and abrasive, the knowledge base for their decision making is richly informed.

Today, the exercise of power in labor unions closely approximates that in other decision-making areas of the society. While there continues to be no major national ideology to support the labor union movement in America, the position of its leaders and their supporting staff is similar to that of other decision makers. In effect, this reduces the uniqueness of the labor union movement and integrates it into the fabric of the total society. The point at issue here, however, is the movement of specialists into the positions of power and influence even in a heretofore unique part of the society, which theoretically should have opted against such influence on an ideological basis.

Although labor union leaders themselves are most often from blue-collar backgrounds, many now obtain college educations and are prepared to compete as idea people.

One of the most notable experiences in the exercise of power involving idea people is the effort to "require" their loyalty. Idea people by the nature of their work and by their occupational sentiment are more loyal to ideas than to each other, than to work environments, or even than to nations. When the basic expressions of ideas and of power are increasingly interrelated, indeed in a labyrinth in the latter part of the twentieth century, it is difficult to understand why there is a need to demand loyalty and why there is overt rejection if not violence against acceptance of loyalty oaths.

Plurality of ideas provides a rich basis for organizing a high quality human enviornment as well as for exercising power with informed dispatch. In a free society there is no higher expression of quality of environment than the open flow of divergent ideas. But societies do not exist in vacuums. With the movement of power and equilibrium among the many societies in the world, the desire, if not need, for unanimity at a specific point in time in history may be great. It is precisely at this point in the last part of the twentieth century that idea people in contrast to old line governmental authority people come into conflict. Action intellectuals as idea people are the new Brahmins—a power elite—but they have not yet obliterated a new charisma. With the continuing demise of charisma and with the growth of idea power, some degree of power conflict over loyalty oaths is in itself a service to the changing society.

Knowledge production and application is what idea people do for urbanized society. The complexities of urbanized societies require the systematic gathering of masses of data and data analysis in the effort to achieve high quality environment for individuals. Research produces much of this body of knowledge and contributes to its analysis. Subsequently their participation in administration for the application of the body of knowledge is essential in operating such a society. Whether in fact this leads to cybernocracy as a new nirvana is a matter of current debate. The answer remains in the future. It is clear in the present that idea people do produce a major body of knowledge and increasingly do participate in the applying of that body of knowledge for society.

The environment in which idea people work is a distinctive one. Its most salient characteristic is a general freedom to create, test, and pursue one's ideas. This atmosphere is dominated by a strong commitment to ideas, a strong reliance on the judgment of one's professional associates, a high degree of stress, and, if one is successful, a high level of financial gratification and professional distinction. The most propitious, challenging, and productive work environments are not those of organization men or "company men." Idea people are more cosmopolitan than local. Above all, they are devoted to their work and give more allegiance to it than to organizations, people, and governments.[1]

Put another way, discretionary use of time is a researcher's primary asset. Indeed for most great imaginative thinkers this is more important than organizational structure, equipment, and relationships with colleagues, although these are also important.[2] The organizational chart for a research laboratory may look like other organizational charts, but it is different. The informal structure in the research organization is ultimately more important than the formal structure. Although the formal structure does exist, it is not a typical bureaucratic hierarchy. The director of a research laboratory,

6

idea work environments

often a vice-president for research, is usually an outstanding idea person in his own right. His office and those directly attached to it, like the administrative services, in effect furnish support for the idea people in productive research. Their primary role is to provide the support services necessary for the creative environment. The directors of research programs have groups or research teams organized under them. Each of the research teams is headed by a coordinator, generally a Ph.D. Within the team structure there is considerable flexibility so that its coordinator and members may organize their projects to get the greatest possible results. The research teams are provided with an appropriate amount of nontechnical back-up staff as aides or assistants in their work.

In industrial research labs a great deal of emphasis is placed on cost factors. As a project develops researchers are kept informed of the potential economic value of their work in relation to its cost. Regular routines are established for research coordinators, research directors, and laboratory directors to meet and discuss the status of projects, the overall accomplishments and the general direction and philosophy of the lab work. In effect in research laboratories the real organizational power comes from the authority of colleagues. Formal organizational structures operate primarily to provide general guidance, individual project integration into the total mission of work, the research facilities, and other aids. Sensitivity to the needs of research staffs is usually insured best by employing researchers as administrators.[3] Research administrators tend in the early years of their administration work, to continue productive research, but the demands of their office soon make this impossible. Consequently in a very short time their colleagues in the research laboratories look upon them increasingly as administrators and less as idea producers. As administrators mature, their administrative duties become their basic responsibility to the organization; if they continue to produce research, it is a secondary function.

idea work environments

Mature research administrators learn to identify basic staff needs and to set priorities. These include: highly satisfying work, professional recognition, informal group membership, equitable financial and status regards, and adequate working conditions.[4] For instance, professional researchers are motivated more by intrinsically satisfying and meaningful work than by material status symbols and high salaries; this set of values is clearly different from the general labor force, but it is an important one for research administrator awareness.

Professional recognition is a matter of critical importance to idea people. Their work is esoteric, isolating, and difficult to communicate—by nature research is unique, and it is often difficult to find a receptive audience. Publication of research must be encouraged both for the dissemination of the findings and for professional recognition. However, it takes a strong sustaining ego on the part of the researcher to be bolstered solely by professional recognition. After these ephemeral but fundamental types of rewards, research administrators do need to concern themselves with financial remuneration and the physical conditions of their research facilities. These items are not unimportant but they are secondary in importance.

Research administrators must also be concerned with the emphasis and direction of research. They must be able to plan for a realistic distribution of work between industrial, governmental, and social needs. This kind of distribution helps sustain strong support for laboratories. Specifically, the research administrator must direct the long-range planning that will produce economically sound research. In other words, the research administrator is continually concerned with financial support, which is easier to obtain if his laboratory produces research that is economically attractive to potential benefactors. Financial needs cause research administrators to be in regular dialogue and communication with the top officials of industry, government, and other areas of society that support research laboratories.

Research administrators are also concerned with recruiting new personnel into the laboratories and with providing the specific focus to training necessary for existing staff, including continuous training, retraining, and up-dated training. Finally, the administrator must provide creative leadership by coordinating the many individual research projects and their products into a total contribution which can be understood and utilized by relevant parties.[5]

The future of research and of idea people in urbanized America is still uncertain. New scientific "breakthroughs" do not follow on a systematic schedule. But the number of dramatic breakthroughs has been so great that, ironically, they have created the need for even more scientific discoveries. Accordingly, in recent decades the federal government has become the primary funding source for research facilities, regardless of whether they are operated by private industry, government laboratories, or universities.[6] While the Congress has many highly trained specialists, most of them are lawyers by profession and are more acquainted with executive and administrative needs. They are not characteristically researchers and have considerable difficulty in perceiving precisely the needs of research-oriented facilities. One important mechanism for funding research programs and facilities is the National Science Foundation. It supports funding for basic research. Other agencies provide funding for more applied and developmental work. Indeed, because of the great complexity of the work environment in research programs and facilities, most of this chapter is devoted to it rather than to the administrative environment in research programs.

In America the federal government is the primary support for much research—even the research carried out in private industry, universities, and related agencies. Some research is conducted in government laboratories, but this is not typical in the United States. In the Soviet Union, by contrast, research work is generally supported by government and carried out in its laboratories rather than in university laboratories or other agencies.[7] Somewhat similarly in Great Britain one finds large government research laboratories staffed by able idea people. The focus of work in these agencies is shifted from time to time in accordance with changing national priorities. For example, in Harwell, England, the government's major atomic energy research establishment employed there approximately fifty-five hundred people in the late 1960s. By the end of the 1960s, after a quarter of a century's work in atomic research, decisions were made to redirect the agency's research from atomic energy to general industrial research. Under its new organization the Harwell Laboratories are intended to pay their own way by contracting to perform research for private industry. Such a new direction has significant and potentially controversial implications for the atmosphere in which research is conducted when a high priority is continually placed on making research findings "public domain" and thereby available to all who are in a position to use them.[8]

Finally, by way of introduction, we reiterate the point that the work environment of idea people is most saliently characterized by freedom. This freedom, however, does not preclude coordination. In the totally unstructured research environment the probability of frustration or low-level productivity is increased. In a totally structured laboratory one is virtually assured of unimaginative work. The highest productivity occurs between these extremes, where freedom and coordination are compatibly integrated and not antithetical.[9]

commitment to ideas

The productive thinker, whether a researcher or an administrator, is committed to idea generation and problem solving. This often leads to a public image of such individuals as "cold" and "remote." As psychologist Roe puts it, "The truth of the matter is that the creative scientist, whatever his field, is very deeply involved emotionally and personally with his work. And, he is himself his own most essential tool."[10] The life of a creative person involves extreme risk and individuality which are difficult for the less committed and creative person to understand. Even within the idea people community there are great differences in how several colleagues will formulate a hypothesis and go about testing it. Individual perception is the essence of the creative environment.

By nature successful idea people must have strong commitments to new orientations. The matter of personal commitment to a hypothesis is one that deserves more consideration than it usually receives. Any man who has gone through the emotional process of developing a new idea, of constructing a new hypothesis, is to some extent, and usually to a large extent, committed to that hypothesis in a very real sense. It is his baby. It is as much his creation as a painting is the personal creation of the painter. True, it stands or falls, is accepted or rejected in the long run on its own merits, but its creator has a personal stake in it. The hazard of the scientist is greater than that of the artist, for the scientist risks a check which is in the public domain in a sense in which art criticism never is. It may even be because of this risk that scientists customarily themselves check their hypotheses as far as they can before they state them publicly. And, indeed, the experienced scientist will continue to check, hoping that if errors are to be found, it will be he who finds them, and hence he who has the chance to make such revisions as may prove adequate or even discard the hypothesis himself. It is not so difficult to discard one if in his efforts at checking he has been able to come up with another one.[11]

There has been some study and much writing about the creative process; most of it is commentary. The one point that is repeatedly observed in the process is the intimately personal character of research. Idea people must have strong motivations and strong egos to continue the risk of research and administrative decision making. Intelligence of course is high among research individuals, but high intelligence alone is insufficient. Important idea people have more than an ordinary amount of curiosity and more than an ordinary amount of ego which they commit and use to sustain themselves in their research.

A personality profile of idea people includes factors like openness to new experience with independence, self-sufficiency, cognition, and perception. They have more than an ordinary amount of desire for creating a new order and for high aesthetic quality. They also have a strong sense of self and an ability for self-discipline. In most cases idea people have a low capacity for social interaction and tend less to gregariousness than most people. Their orientation is to things and ideas rather than to people, except in the social sciences and administration, where other people become their subjects. In these cases, however, the emotional commitment is to people as subjects of a study rather than to people as people. Finally, the idea person is favorably committed to taking calculated risks but less as a matter of chance than as an alternative within a range of probabilities.[12]

The worlds and the work of many great creative people are so isolated and private that even their names remain for the most part anonymous.[13] For example, music composers have little contact even with conductors, performers, and audiences. On the first night of a performance of a composer's new work, he may be invited as a guest and introduced to the audience. But that is an exception; in the creative process, the individual is usually remote, isolated, and even unknown.

cosmopolitans and locals

In work environments involving ideas, there are two kinds of creative people, namely cosmopolitans and locals. Cosmopolitans have stronger commitments to ideas as "things" in and for themselves. Locals have stronger commitments to their group.[14] Cosmopolitans generally have less power than locals in the immediate work environment. They must "sell" their ideas. Put another way, cosmopolitans have less firm loyalty than locals. For cosmopolitans the judgments of experts and colleagues in other agencies may be more significant than those of fellow workers in their immediate work environment.

Cosmopolitans are high producers and publishers. They seek environments which give them maximum free time to follow their own interests rather than those most specified by an employer. In universities cosmopolitans seek light teaching loads and maximum individual research and travel time. In industry and government cosmopolitans seek the right to publish, attend professional meetings, and to freely present the ideas generated from their research.

The ideal research staff has a delicate balance of both cosmopolitans and locals. Too many cosmopolitans can leave an employer with too few workers interested in the agency and its needs. Too many locals will lead to stagnation and insufficient innovation. Employers must continually "sell" cosmopolitans on "company consciousness." Creative people need to see the relation of their work to the welfare of their employer. In fact, whether their primary concern is for their work or for the agency, the welfare of their work is ultimately related to that of their employer.

ideas and the age cycle

While the commitment to an idea is an infectious thing, the young idea person may flounder in doubt until his priorities are firmly identified. Particularly in the research and development laboratories, administrators are challenged, while not being overly directive, to facilitate the identification of their younger researchers with a project. In some cases this may involve assigning an area of work that is specific and yet not overly narrow. The subject of inquiry that will encourage a young researcher to read extensively, consult with colleagues, and examine the subject from many different points of view must be identified. In some cases an older researcher may serve as an appropriate mentor. For this reason post-doctoral training is attractive. The younger researcher needs an environment that will enable him to grow and achieve maximum recognition and opportunity for publication. With the proper professional guidance, the young researcher should be free to stand alone and to chart his own direction by his late twenties or early thirties.[15]

The administrator has another very different but equally important problem: the older researcher. At this stage in life some idea people tend to be "burned out." They should have a well-developed desire for direction, self-confidence, and risk taking; new courses, a sabbatical leave, or a move to a different area of the laboratory may provide appropriate new challenges. The desire for inquiry should be firmly established at this stage in life, and the individual may simply need some stimulus to rekindle his desire to explore the unknown. This problem also exists for administrators; hence, experienced administrators in their forties and fifties may move from industry to a university to oversee a research project in an area that offers a new and different challenge.

professional relationships

The desire for excellence and leadership in one's profession are important forces motivating idea people: they have an all-consuming commitment to ideas. Their work environment is an important sustaining force in their creative work, and the crucial part of this environment is the researcher's relationship with his colleagues. It is probable that the search for one's true colleagues is nearly a life-long process beginning in adolescence and continuing through the fullness of one's career.[16] Defining what is excellence and what is leadership is difficult at best. An idea person relies heavily on the judgment of trusted colleagues as research complexities increase. Ideas are tested again and again and tried out on colleagues prior to general presentation to clients or the public, where they finally succeed or fail.

The world of colleagues is the environment for testing. It too is a precarious environment. It is surrounded by critical competition and social distance. In highest essence the nature of the creative world is the competition to achieve higher quality or to produce an excellent product, whether it be a research breakthrough or an administrative accomplishment. In fact the competition is more between ideas than it is personal, but professional competition and personal competition are hard to differentiate at the point of critical assessment. Accordingly one seeks out one's professional allies, whether they are cabinet members in the government, board members of the corporation, or members of a scientific agency.[17] In the broad sweep of things the products of creative thinkers are gaining prestige in America. Contemporary society is increasingly aware of its dependence on idea people, but the norms of society have not yet established new ideas as popular or easy to accept.[18]

Even in those administrative areas where new agreements and new understandings seem, by definition, to be the purpose of work, as for example in the case of the State Department, new ideas are not popular. There is an abiding effort to maintain the status quo. Fresh new ideas are unsettling. There are, in fact, intermediate levels of achievement in most idea work environments which offer moderate measures of security as a "reward" to those who will "water down" new ideas and not pursue them too aggressively. Indeed in the professional world a quasi-normative and bureaucratic posture tends to inhibit the production, existence, and communication of ideas. In some cases the intermediate achievement levels may take the character of academic cartels where scholars refine an old idea rather than develop new ones.[19] There are quasi-bureaucratic task forces to which people may be appointed which allow limited innovation, that is change within the guidelines of an official position.[20] In the State Department, for example, there are places which enable middle-range bureaucrats to defer making any decisions as long as possible, particularly when they involve new ideas. On the one hand this may be rationalized as using appropriate caution to study positions thoroughly because of their potentially far reaching implications. On the other hand it may often be due to intellectual timidity.

The courage for innovation, creativity, and liberalism may be fostered by a high degree of satisfactory professional relations among colleagues. The degrading judgments of one's colleagues are far more damning to a new idea than the assertions of candor, whether laudatory or negative, by the general public. Similarly the sustaining praise of colleagues provides sufficient courage to withstand public or nonprofessional criticism by persons whose competence in the subject is limited.[21]

A further expression of in-group and colleague relationships is found in the multiple authoring of research reports and books.[22] There has been an increasing trend toward collaboration on the part of American research people. Not only are two authors contributing their ideas, but three, four, five or larger numbers are joining in publication of a single work. In critical new areas this spreads or shares the risk. Substantively it may express more aggressive and critical work in formulating hypotheses and much more aggressive and critical work of collecting data, analyzing data, and examining the results as they are finally interpreted and argued to support or reject hypotheses. Furthermore, as the body of knowledge proliferates, it is increasingly difficult for any one specialist to come close to approximating the so-called Renaissance Man's grasp of the broad range of intellectual concerns. Intense collaboration among several idea people at any particular time may substantively strengthen in depth and increase in breadth the competency of performance on the subject at hand. The reasons for multiple authorship are several, and further investigation is needed to fully understand the reasons for it. However, the importance of the subject here is its illustration of the growing complexities of the atmosphere in which research is conducted and the increasing interaction among specialists in different areas.

As areas of professional interest expand, colleagues outside of immediate subject areas are identified. This is partly a function of interdisciplinary and multidisciplinary investigations and partly a function of the increasingly complex relationship between research and administration.[23]

The idea-oriented businessman and the idea-oriented professor may in some cases experience little social distance; in some cases they may even be colleagues. The research professor's world of work may now commonly include a campus laboratory, an industrial or government conference room, and a visit to a meeting or seminar in another nation in the space of a few hours, days, or weeks. This kind of work environment is similar to that of an aggressive business or government executive whose desk may in reality be more a briefcase while on a plane-hopping mission than a piece of physical furniture in the home office.

This reporting of the work environment is no brief for or against it. It is to make it clear that idea people have some common work situations even when their subjects are vastly different.

The trend to evaluate the work of professionals on the basis of "productivity" whether their work is research, development, or administration has increased in recent years.[24] In the professional world one is typically given freedom to set one's own goals rather than have them be set by an institution. This is true for executives, artists, researchers, development personnel, and others. But the freedom is not without its limitations. If one is not sufficiently "productive," stockholders may remove the executive from his office, critics may see the artist's work as being irrelevant or of low quality, reviewers may find the researcher's work inadequate and the product developed obsolete. Freedom for goal setting is difficult rather than easy: it disproportionately places the onus of responsibility on the individual. Professional friends may encourage goal setting that is realistic while clients of the public may expect too much or too little. The drive for goal accomplishment for most creative thinkers means their work is never done—at least not to their satisfaction for quality and excellence. They may frustrate themselves more by being overachievers rather than underachievers. The sage and moderating judgments of colleagues may reduce frustration and in a meaningful way express the adequacy of goal achievement.

The arena of colleagueship is characterized by growth, development, and change. One's colleagues at a given point in his career will probably be different from the colleagues at other points in his career. The changing of colleagues provides for idea stimulation. Earlier colleagues may continue as friends, and friends from earlier periods in one's life may become colleagues. Personal friendship and professional association are typically different although not mutually exclusive.[25]

Independent invention outside of collaboration is declining. Some individuals concentrate on the refinement and further illucidation of so-called established great theories or major administrative positions. This is both a collective and collaborative process. It develops "schools of thought," traditions of thought, and patterns of administration.

The independent invention is difficult to measure accurately due to limited statistics. Nevertheless, it appears clearly to be on the decline. In 1920 the U.S. Patent Office recorded 7.7 patent applications per 10,000 citizens. By the 1950s the rate had dropped to 4.6 Industry has tried to stimulate independent innovation by offering prizes and using suggestion boxes, but with little success.[26] Colleagueship and the environment of cooperative enterprise is characteristic of the creative world in contemporary America. This is to a considerable extent a consequence of the bigness of science.

stress and strain

In many respects the work environments of research and administrative people are glamorous. Scientific breakthroughs receive a great deal of dramatic fanfare; for example, the manned moon landings of the 1970s and major administrative moves like the American presidential visit to China in 1972 received a great deal of publicity. Such notable events build the prestige of idea people, but most of the real life situations of the world of creative thinkers differ both in degree and kind. The world of ideas is in fact characterized by loneliness—stress-ridden loneliness. Researchers, even in small groups, pursue in an esoteric manner the relentless quest for new insights. Even when most of their work is of a nonclassified nature, the general public could hardly care less. Seldom could the public be easily informed even if it cared. In most cases, until a considerable amount of developmental work follows an idea breakthrough, the importance of the intellectual contribution remains and receives little public recognition.

In a strikingly similar fashion, the work of top executives is lonely. After the various councils and advisory groups have submitted their reports and after the mass of known data has been analyzed and presented, the final task of synthesis and decision making rests with one individual or a very small group of individuals. This is a risky, lonely course, regardless of whether the goal is to increase dividends for stockholders in industry, to achieve a new treaty for international relations, to create new health delivery programs for the poor, or to provide more housing for the needy. The emotional stress and strain in idea work is excessive. Only individuals with exceptional stability and enormous amounts of energy can long sustain themselves in the intense world of creativity. There is a high incidence of neurological disorders, indeed even suicides, among idea people.[27]

The stress and strain of work in the world of ideas is intensified by the urgency for creativity. Young idea persons normally do not complete post-graduate training until their middle or late twenties. In most research and administrative positions the development or implementing of new ideas normally takes two to three years. One may anticipate that the chance of success is one in ten or less. Study of the idea

idea work environments

experience reveals that major contributions in some fields are made as early as the late twenties and in almost all fields by or before the early forties. The creative environment is, therefore, characterized by a sense of urgency. One must make a major contribution quickly or the probability of making such a contribution at all is sharply diminished. High achievement is reached by only a few. While the "fun" of idea production may continue, outstanding achievement is pock marked by intense competition and stress.[28]

Medical studies of idea people give a more precise indication of the emotional problems which arise at different stages in their careers. In general individuals who enter such careers pay a high price personally—and so do their families.[29] It already has been reported that idea people typically manifest different personality characteristics from the general population. They tend in the early years of life to be more isolated, less physically active, and more concerned with ideas. Even in early life some manifest more than an ordinary amount of personality disorganization—many are obsessed by work. In fact, many professionals both in research and administration find it difficult to differentiate work and leisure. Their work is a way of life and tends to be never ending. This condition alone is sufficient to explain much of the neurosis experienced by creative people.[30]

The compulsive work orientation and the difficulty in differentiating work and leisure create family tensions. In the professional training at the college level, married graduate students often live in cramped quarters, and some have poverty-level incomes. Upon completion of study and entry into occupational work, a creative person's standard of living usually improves greatly, but it can vary considerably depending on what part of the idea world one enters. In any event, his absorption in work may increase drastically, and his wife and children may see little of him. If both husband and wife are professionals, they may see little of each other and their children less of either. Under such conditions family life is often unsatisfactory and divorce is frequent.[31]

In this complex world further investigation should be made of the following subjects:

1. The economic and psychological stresses on the lives of young idea persons
2. The factors which consciously and unconsciously determine the research careers of young scientists
3. The interplay of forces which determine the personality and research maturation of idea people
4. The relation of later life stresses to earlier life stresses in the career of creative persons
5. The impact of stress on the researcher's approach to science and to investigative controversy
6. How unconscious symbolic factors and theories can distort logic and judgment even for scientists of high ability[32]

Kubie's studies of personality characteristics in scientific work environments indicate that, in order to obtain privacy, researchers do from time to time resort to locking their doors in order to avoid colleagues who drift in to talk less about scientific phenomena than about personal problems. The frustration of personal problems is not restricted to the younger idea people. It is manifested among the older individuals as well. The creative environment is characterized by prolonged frustration and uncertainty which from time to time break even strong and experienced persons.

The background of the idea person is usually that of an intelligent, if not gifted, child, who displayed some neurotic tendencies and aggressive psychosexual development in early years.[33] Such individuals are usually exceedingly stimulated by one adult, a "significant other" who turns them from the child-like concerns of athletics and social life to a more bookish, intellectual pattern of inquiry. In his adolescent years, the potential idea person becomes very selective in his behavior, putting enormous emotional and intellectual effort into work-related activity to the near exclusion of many other kinds of human activities. When in a few years the life of intellectual inquiry is entered vocationally, the commitment is "total." Other personality manifestations are subjected to conscious and unconscious aspirations for intellectual cravings. But even brilliant success in idea work does not solve or abate the unconscious personality craving which tends to be suppressed for the intellectual life. So much is the above the case that serious depression may follow notable success. Kubie says this is because the deeper personality problems are left unsolved by intellectual curiosity and success.

In the informal and formal socialization for career life, adults are notoriously poor in explaining to their children and to their students the psychosocial characteristics of work environments. Similarly students are poorly prepared to observe these subtle, and sometimes not so subtle, personality problems of active intellectuals, be they mentors or not. The work environment of idea people, in and of itself, is less seductive and more a situation into which younger persons gravitate due to personal factors than by force of society. It is, nevertheless, wasteful in a manpower sense and unfortunate for individuals involved when they are even temporarily recruited into this type of environment and find that they do not have the personality to survive there. The dropout or noncompletion rate in the graduate schools is extremely high—in some cases approaching 50 percent. Idea training in professional schools is structured so that entry is more restrictive and drop out rates are lower, yet they are significant.

The work environment of idea people requires the capacity to deal with frustrating personal situations as well as with extraordinary intelligence. Indeed, the malady of personality problems is irritated more than ameliorated by the work environment. Kubie asserts that there is insufficient understanding of the neurotic pressure which research exerts on the young idea person. The quest for originality may in fact be a disguise for unconscious hostility to authority. It may be that the effort to achieve originality is misunderstood both by the professor and his student. The young researcher may, in fact, be having considerable difficulty in understanding the accomplishments and achievements of those who preceded him. In these cases, the drive for new discoveries may be reckless cover-ups.[34]

The ego involvement of creative people is excessive. It is manifested at an early age and continues throughout an individual's career. Yet some great investigators remain most ambiguous and vague, Kubie asserts, because unconsciously they are unable to experience fully the success or trauma of seeing their own scientific questions fully answered.[35]

stress and invasion of privacy

In the creative world there is a strong belief that the openness and dissemination in both research and administration must be maintained. When administrators deal in classified information, the probability of a credibility gap increases. When researchers work under security or censorship, they feel that the situation is often unethical and, perhaps even more important, wasteful. Failure to disseminate research findings may cause different researchers to conduct unrelated studies of subjects. This situation may deter the cumulative building on information of others. Nevertheless, in contemporary societies it appears that there will be social pressure, if not political pressure, for classification and secrecy from time to time.[36] This pressure on idea people to accommodate some degree of classification and secrecy, thereby altering the conditions under which they work, provides stress for individuals and strain in the professional atmosphere.

Viewed from the opposite perspective, the norms of intellectual work are so oriented to inquiry, both for research and administrative purposes, that the investigators themselves are often accused of invading the privacy of others. Biological scientists and administrators of hospitals and medical centers have for long periods of time, at least indirectly if not directly, subjected their clients to scrutiny, study, and investigation above and beyond diagnosis and treatment. Without speaking in defense of idea people or in defense of client privacy, one must concede that it is difficult to define where diagnosis and treatment stops and where investigation for the further production of knowledge begins. In any event growing out of that difficult and complex work situation other investigators and administrators have capitalized on these fuzzy distinctions to subject clients to considerable observation and questioning even through interviews and questionnaires on the pretense of diagnosis and treatment. The tension that exists between society and idea people in the area of secrecy and privacy invasion has increased. The issues concern not only data collection and analysis but information dissemination. In addition to investigation areas, privacy in administrative areas is of critical importance in employment interviewing, social welfare screening, law enforcement investigations, and other areas.

In America creative people are forced to accept the notion that some degree of consent is necessary.[37] Some basic inquiry is frustrated, if not eliminated, by revealing to subjects sufficient information to obtain their consent, because the basic research situation in some cases is fundamentally changed when the subject is aware of his or her participation in research. Nevertheless, issues of individual human dignity and the right of the individual to decide for himself what others should know about his thoughts, feelings, and personal life have reached such a point of controversy that increasing ethics and policy have been established to bring equity to both clients and idea people alike.[38] In the government publication *Privacy and Behavioral Research* one reads as follows:

> Basically then, protection of privacy in research is assured first by securing the informed consent of the subject. When the subject cannot be completely informed, the consent must be based on trust in the scientist and the institution sponsoring him. In any case the scientist and his sponsoring institution must insure privacy by the maintenance of confidentiality.

| *idea people*

In the end, the fact must be accepted that human behavioral research will at times produce discomfort to some subjects, and will entail a partial invasion of their privacy. Neither the principle of privacy nor the need to discover new knowledge can supervene universally. As with other conflicting values in our society, there must be consent, adjustment and compromise, with the decision as to which value is to govern in a given instance determined by a weighing of the cost and the gains—the cost in privacy, the gain in knowledge. The decision cannot be made solely by the investigator, who normally has a vested interest in his own research program, but be a positive concern of his scientific peers and the institution which sponsors his work.[39]

The stress and strain on both investigators and administrators in matters of privacy and secrecy is illustrated in situations like Project Camelot.[40] This was to have been a major policy and scientific study of causes of revolution and insurgency in underdeveloped countries. The project was funded by the U.S. Army at a cost between $4 and $6 million over a three- to four-year period. Camelot was conceived in 1963. It started in Chile and was to have been extended from Latin America to Asia, Africa and Europe. The project was killed by the secretary of defense even before the first Chilean phase was completed. Among researchers there were credibility problems from the start because of the Defense Department funding. Early on, there developed strong opposition from the Department of State, which reflected citizen opposition in Chile which was directed against the American embassy in Santiago. Ultimately President Johnson decided that no government-sponsored research would be accepted in foreign areas if in the secretary of state's judgment it would adversely affect U.S. foreign relations. The real issue in Camelot was the invasion of a nation's privacy.

The social circumstances of idea people in American society never have been better than in recent years. Those circumstances, nevertheless, are not all positive and indeed in some situations leave much to be desired. Their importance and contribution to the urbanized society is paramount. Generally society awards idea people with high status; most receive substantial financial rewards, and they also receive many nontangible benefits. In spite of conflict over invasion of privacy and questions concerning credibility, the work environment of idea people is propitious both in the administrative and investigative areas. Accordingly, there are many opportunities for personal gratification in professional achievement. In 1968 the income patterns of 298,000 scientists reported in the *National Register* showed a median annual salary of $13,200. In the highest decile the remuneration was over $21,500 and in the lowest decile below $8,500.[41] Economists had the highest median salary and agricultural scientists the lowest median. Similarly economists recorded the highest upper decile salary and the lowest was reported for biological scientists. While it is widely recognized that idea people are not primarily motivated by economic considerations, administrators realize that there is a critical need for financial equity and economic reward for them.[42] Moreover, administrators must be careful to evaluate merit fairly and recognize it with pay increases. There may be several hierarchical categories in the research environment where the top salaries are open, enabling individuals with different status to have equal salaries if circumstances justify it.[43]

It has been observed on many occasions that idea people have an exceptionally high degree of mobility. Moreover, their mobility allows them to seek the most advantageous employment, which includes financial opportunity. The map in Figure 6.1, reflects gross differences in the geographical location of scientists. The Middle Atlantic states and the Pacific states have the largest proportion of scientists. They are followed by the East North Central and the South Atlantic states. In the lowest areas are: East South Central, Mountain, and West South Central states.[44]

Administrators receive the highest salaries in particular, and other amenities of office in general, among the idea people—and indeed for the national population. It is difficult to obtain complete comparative data on the remunerations of administrators. Some cases, however, illustrate the situation. A top executive may sign a contract with a major corporation for a salary of several hundred thousand dollars a year for three to five years, plus thousands of dollars (often as much as $50,000 to $75,000) annually for the rest of his life. Viewed from another perspective, an executive with a major corporation may retire from a position paying several hundred thousand dollars annually and retirement benefit in the lower five-figure range; however with annual "deferred payment" his income will still be in the upper five-figure range.[45] In addition executives in private industry may receive remuneration in the form of options to buy stock at or below current market levels. Other financial benefits for administrators include such fringe benefits as paid memberships in clubs, free medical care, use of company lawyers and accountants, specialized facilities for entertaining customers, the use of private recreation areas, scholarships for children, and the provision of company automobiles. From a financial point of view security for creative people in private industry is greater than in the other areas of idea people employment. Other techniques to maintain research people are also used so that ideas cannot be easily "pirated" to another company.[46]

In a society with few class distinctions an earned title can provide a high degree of personal satisfaction. Titles like professor, minister, scientist, doctor, lawyer, engineer, physician, and president all carry high status. Generally they bring deference and respect. Some individuals are literally frightened and inhibited when in the presence of a great scientist, professor, minister, or physician. Some professional people studiously opt not to use their titles, in many cases reflecting a reverse snobbery.[47] Nevertheless, even the opportunity for a title on one's door, business card, or publication affords an important kind of remuneration in a society that does not have inherited titles.

Professional and economic rewards do not come quickly; many creative thinkers never achieve either. Generally most who reach the highest levels do so rapidly and early in their careers. Ironically there is a considerable measure of gratification and remuneration which is not a matter of luck, but a matter of life circumstances beyond the individual's control. To a great extent the investigator or administrator who reaches the pinnacle of his field is a product of the time and place as much as a product of his own initiative.[48] The young scientist's future is often determined by forces beyond his control. There is, in fact, a "star" system similar to that of the stage. There is also a similar pattern of mental illness between scientists and actors.[49]

The matter of gratification and reward has an intrinsically illusive nature about it. Research directors and administrators discover that creative people can be motivated only to a limited extent by appealing to status symbols. In effect the most important status symbols are covert ones—from colleagues—rather than overtly from an institution or from society. Consequently, directors and administrators in the idea work environment must give careful and subtle attention to the reward system—both intrinsic and extrinsic.[50]

This difficulty in pleasing creative thinkers is increased by the creative person's lack of appreciative identification with his employer. Whether in industry or in other kinds of agencies, they tend, as previously observed, to be more cosmopolitan than local in their orientation. Business and industry are particularly challenged to demonstrate that the rewards they offer are more than crassly material and that providing material service to mankind is an important source of gratification, achievement, and remuneration.[51] Business and industry are moving to develop a milieu in which publishing and other scholarly presentations are not only provided but encouraged. At the same time creative people employed in these agencies are encouraged to seek professional fulfillment in seeing their ideas used for profitable products for mankind.[52]

table 6.1
distribution of scientists by regions

regions	percent
Pacific (Alaska, California, Hawaii, Oregon, Washington) . . .	15
Mountain (Arizona, Colorado, Idaho, Montana, Nevada, New Mexico, Utah, Wyoming).	6
West North Central (Iowa, Kansas, Minnesota, Missouri, Nebraska, North Dakota, South Dakota)	7
West South Central (Arkansas, Louisiana, Oklahoma, Texas)	8
East North Central (Illinois, Indiana, Michigan, Ohio, Wisconsin)	17
East South Central (Alabama, Kentucky, Mississippi, Tennessee)	3
New England (Connecticut, Maine, Massachusetts, New Hampshire, Rhode Island, Vermont)	7
Middle Atlantic (New Jersey, New York, Pennsylvania)	20
South Atlantic (Delaware, District of Columbia, Georgia, Florida, Maryland, North Carolina, South Carolina, Virginia, West Virginia)	15
Foreign Areas	2

Source: National Register of Scientific and Technical Personnel, 1970.

summary

The work environments for idea people are unique. They can at best be only superficially described. Many of their most salient characteristics defy conventional written description. This is one of the reasons that there is so much difficulty in communicating the real nature of the intellectual life to students. Creative people are not seduced into intellectual pursuits by a mysterious force. They are attracted

idea work environments

to this life by the subjects of their work, by opportunities for freedom, and by social status.

To say that the work environment of idea people involves more commitment to ideas than to employers, more loyalty to profession than even to families, much stress and strain in the search for ideas, professional conflict, and gratification from achievement and reward for service to society is to give a shorthand explanation of the much deeper meaning and character of the environment. The creative environment is a curiosity existing within the material urbanized society with so much functional importance and yet in most other ways appearing to be such a "misfit" in this time and place.

In a society where individuality so often seems lost and conformity so often required, the creative environment is unique. In the creative world the individual is "king"— indeed the individual is so much recognized and so little structure is provided to guide performance that more than an ordinary amount of frustration is commonplace.

The contributions of idea people most readily conjured in the mind of the general public concern material things. They include items like automobiles, penicillin, hospitals, airplanes, computers, refrigerators, bombs, television, books, and thousands of other things which make life in our fast moving society possible.[1] The publicity that these kinds of contributions get has led social critics to call our society materialistic, but creative people have made far greater contributions than these. They involve both basic and applied research in software and hardware. Indeed the contributions range from the arts through the social sciences, to the material technologies.

Probably one of the most dramatic events to introduce new knowledge to the general public was the atomic bombing of Hiroshima during World War II. This startling event brought the work of scientists to the attention of the average American citizen with an electrifying immediacy. It elevated scientists to the most promient positions in government. It also quickened their professional sense of social responsibility for society's survival and for human quality of environment. The obscure were at once made heros, or antiheroes. The reward of highest recognition was, however, juxtaposed with anxiety and guilt.[2] With this type of major contribution

7

the contributions of idea people

scientists like J. Robert Oppenheimer expressed for many a feeling which continues to the present: namely, "In some sense which no vulgarity, no humor, no over-statement can quite extinguish, the physicists have known sin and this is a knowledge they cannot lose."[3]

Until the actual explosion of the atomic bomb in World War II, American scientists had implicitly, if not explicitly, generally adhered to a belief in progress through science. There was something of an uncritical and unquestioning notion that science was inevitably for the good of mankind. Scientists, and other creative people, wrestled vehemently over issues of basic and applied research, but seldom questioned what they expected was the general good of knowledge.

After seeing the "fruits" of much creative energy devastate Hiroshima, creative people adopted a new and persistent attitude toward their work. Policy molding and decision making based on research had not been a paramount responsibility of research and other creative people. Now men like Linus Pauling and Edward Teller make presentations and debates concerning, for example, test-ban treaties. Creative people have used their newly won prestige to guide the development and use as well as the production of new ideas. Increasingly top scientists become career bureaucrats devoting full time to the use of ideas. Others participate on ad hoc committees giving forceful and independent direction to idea use in policy areas.[4]

Contemporary research and development is directly related to the gross national product. Both basic and applied research are critical components of a responsive and growing economy. They make direct contributions to the national defense, to growing industries, and to the future development of knowledge.[5]

Creative people have moved into positions of power through administration. For instance, some of them have become involved in politics and have been elected to top political offices.[6] One example is The Lincoln Center for the Performing Arts in New York City. The center encourages and supports new ideas in the arts and education. It is a concrete expression of confidence in man's survival and expresses the enduring values of civilization.[7]

Another measure of the creative activity of the new intellectuals is found in the meetings and publications of the American Association of the Advancement of Science. For over one hundred years, this association has reflected both the subtle and major shifts in scientific thought in America.[8] It has been in the vanguard of experimentation and creative research. For instance, its 1970 president, Athelstan Spilhaus, was a leader in the development of the "sea-grant college system" and of the Minnesota Experimental City program.[9]

The role of complex computer-based command and control systems in research has become increasingly important. Interdisciplinary teams on large-scale projects involving systems engineers, computer programmers, operations researchers, and related areas of expertise to handle problems relating to a wide variety of subjects, problems as diverse as the timely production, transportation, and distribution of new products like sperm, to biological warfare. The shapes of urbanized society from environmental pollution to euthanasia are due to persistent and increasing idea contributions.

A few examples of the new products and processes idea people have produced should illustrate the importance of manpower-training policy. These examples most certainly are not exhaustive, but they will provide the kind of information necessary for policy considerations.

decision making

Decision makers are influenced by a variety of factors including: data banks, game theory, simulation models, automation, cybernation, intelligence strategies, social criticism, and increasingly less by individual power and charisma. Decision making has clearly become more than a function of individual judgment; it includes the full range of intelligence sources.

Simulation and business games have become increasingly important for American decision making.[10] Simulation techniques are not new. Many law schools have used moot courts to train young lawyers and education departments have used laboratory schools for teacher training for many years. However, it is only recently that specific simulation games have been developed for training decision makers in management. By the 1970s specialists have contributed well over one hundred different business simulations that have been used for training in all types of industries, agencies, and university business departments in the United States and in many other places throughout the world.

Another new approach to training decision makers is illustrated by the "California Tomorrow" plan.[11] This is an interdisciplinary task-force approach that includes the fields of politics and journalism, city planning and architecture, ecology and business. Unlike the traditional problem-solving approach of taking individual components separately, which often results in compounding the problem, the California Tomorrow plan focuses on interrelationships among elements of a problem.

During World War II the need for intelligence in governmental decision making was vastly accelerated. The Office of Strategic Services was established and at its peak operated with more than twelve thousand persons. When this intelligence procuring office was disbanded in 1945, after four years of operation, its total cost had been $135 million.[12]

Following World War II there continued to be a keen awareness of the need for intelligence in governmental decision making. Ultimately the Central Intelligence Agency was established by the National Security Act of 1947. Much of its initial personnel came from the old Office of Strategic Services. Systematic procurement of intelligence continues to be a part of the government's decision-making tools, which include careful scrutiny of newspapers, books, learned and technical publications, official reports of government proceedings, radio and television, novels and plays, and so forth. Clandestine agents are also used to collect data. The contribution of the intelligence service has become so established that a new professional occupational category of intelligence officer is being created.[13]

From the turn of the century to the mid-1930s creative thinkers developed scientific methods of management. Leadership in this area was provided by engineers, particularly Frederick Taylor. Taylor's scientific management technique focused on time-and-motion studies, and production was significantly increased by application of this method of organization and decision making. By the mid-1930s the influence of this school of thought had grown to the point where the *Bulletin of the Taylor Society* and of the *Society of Industrial Engineers* was published. Like many new methods, it was utimately pushed to excess, and it precipitated a counter-movement known as human relations in industry.

Law was an independent approach to decision making in the early days of the nation, but since the 1960s, it has come to reflect business attitudes.[14] Indeed, by the 1960s the Bar had become so closely associated with business interests that it was difficult to distinguish them. Certainly this was in contrast with its lack of alignment to labor, agriculture, and other interest groups. Lawyers constituted during this period the single largest occupational group in the federal Congress, which in effect meant that business, and generally big business, had a direct influence on governmental decision making. As in the case of professional reaction to scientific managers, professional opposition to this situation grew. By the 1970s a movement of young lawyers shifted away from big business to represent minority groups and espouse a variety of social issues. It is far too soon to know if this will constitute a new direction and new contribution to law but it does represent a countermovement against the rather incestuous relationship that has developed between law and business.

Some creative people have participated in attempts to influence decision making through petitions, appeals, dissent,

the contributions of idea people

and demonstrations. For example, in the late 1950s over two thousand scientists in the United States, in response to a call by Linus Pauling, signed an appeal asking for an international test-ban agreement.[15] Similarly in 1972 the Ivy League college and university presidents signed a letter to President Nixon demanding a complete withdrawal of American military forces from Vietnam.[16] Scientists have participated in organizations like SANE. And on March 4, 1969, they participated in a research moratorium. On that day they discussed the moral uses of ideas and the quality of environment through the use of ideas.

Visual and literary artists have contributed to decision making via social critic roles.[17] For example visual artists have developed satiric, sardonic views of the contemporary scene reflecting protest and dissent. Drawings from an exhibition titled "The Poison Pen," at the School of Visual Arts Gallery in Manhattan reflect this dissent. The intent of such social criticism is to stir the consciousness of both decision makers and the population at large. The criticism is against anti-humanitarian behavior patterns and for or toward higher quality human existance.

In literature the concern for social responsibility is an old one.[18] Marcus Klein's, *After Alienation: American Novels in the Mid-Century* (Cleveland: World Publishing Co., 1964); *Ihab Hassan's Radical Innocence: The Contemporary American Novel* (Princeton: Princeton University Press, 1961) or Jerry H. Bryant's "The Last of the Social Protest Writers," *Arizona Quarterly* 19 (Winter, 1963), pp. 315-325, are a few noteworthy examples of social protest embodied in literary criticism. These works on American literature describe the critical content which is part of building the mood of a nation and particularly of its creative people. These artists feel that their primary role is to stimulate social responsibility rather than entertain.

Prose has only been one medium of literary protest. Poems by LeRoi Jones and Allen Ginsberg are two examples of other types of literary protest.[19]

In both of these cases a divisive mood is set. Some people are "turned on" and others, with equal vehemance, "turned off." They are indeed written as a countermovement to the conformist society of the 1950s and early 1960s. They are abrasive and offensive in words and in thought to the "proper" middle class. They are a part of the "tell-it-like-it-is" movement which calls society generally and decision makers particularly to confront the maladies of the many who are racked by material poverty and alienation in this society of affluence. In a less than congenial way, this type of idea person has contributed much to the quickening of decision making and to opening new areas of consideration for decision making.

In addition there is a large body of science fiction literature which by mid-century was making a broad impact on professional people and citizens generally. It set the mood for new directions, new challenges, and new decisions. The titles from science fiction magazines illustrate the stage set for new decision making: *Cosmic Stories, Fantasy Fiction, Imagination, Other World, Planet Stories, Science Fiction Quarterly, Scientific Detective Monthly, Unknown Worlds,* and *Worlds Beyond.*[20] This body of literature continues to proliferate both in books and in articles.

Another very different kind of research has been conducted by a Smithsonian bird-banding project in the Pacific Ocean area. This ornithological research project has made a basic contribution to knowledge of bird migration patterns in that part of the world. The project, however, was funded by the U.S. Department of Defense. Its relation to chemical and biological warfare research is unclear—clouded at best. When the project started in 1963 the Department of Defense contracted for an initial funding of $2.8 million to the Smithsonian Institution to carry out the work. What was a basic biological survey for the Smithsonian Institution was officially reported as applied research for the Department of Defense. The Army said it wanted to know disease distributions which might affect the health of servicemen and civilians in the area, the impact of military installations on bird populations, and possible bird-aircraft collision problems.[21]

The research from the Smithsonian's point of view was never "classified." While the Department of Defense did suppress the publication of some reports, the project by 1969 had produced some forty-five scientific papers which were published.

These illustrations demonstrate that idea research involves conflict, disagreements, and different meanings for different people in society. Indeed, what might be basic research for one part of the idea community may be applied for another. What might be unclassified for some idea people may become a classified subject for others. As the contributions of idea people proliferate and become an ever major part of the way of life of urbanized societies, support, surveillance, and utilization continue to be controversial components of the contributing process.

Creative individuals from all fields of endeavor have contributed to administrative decision making. Their contributions run the gamut—from systematic decision-making models using game theory to the promulgation of ideas which stretch the minds of men in new directions leaving them dissatisfied with the old ways and challenged by new ways.

computers, cybernetics, and society

Idea people build computers. The first computer was constructed at the University of Pennsylvania in 1946.[22] They are largely an outgrowth of World War II research. The computer has had rapid acceptance and is now used extensively in all kinds of industry and research ranging from banking to guided missiles and space vehicles—and the computer is still in its infancy. Data banks are being established to support research at a number of locations, and a national data bank has been proposed.[23] The idea of a national data bank was supported in the mid-1960s by the Social Science Research Council and by government task forces. The primary use for such a facility would be to support basic statistical research by scholars and agency personnel. Such a bank ideally would bring together information from the Census Bureau, the Internal Revenue Service, the Social Security Administration, and other agencies which collect large bodies of data concerning citizens. It would offer many advantages, for example, in the investigation of poverty and of economic malfunctions.

There is considerable fear that a national data bank would in fact constitute a major invasion of privacy. Critics feel that such a massive computerized body of data would bring "Big Brother" into existence before 1984. The House Government Operations Committee's Special Subcommittee on Investigation of Privacy, in 1966, held three days of hearings on the national data bank situation. Among the witnesses was Vance Packard, author of *The Naked Society*. The thrust of the witnesses' testimony and the conclusion of the committee displayed a distrust of such a data bank. This idea has not yet been implemented.

Our computerized society continues its advance even without a national data bank. Computers are increasingly used in banking, for example. Money as we now use it may vanish: computerized banking techniques can make possible automatic credit transfers, and credit cards and computers will make possible checkless and cashless banking systems. Police departments have begun to use computers in their work. Law enforcement will be strengthened by the use of computers. Police patrol cars will be connected by radio to computer centers for attaining instant information on crime suspects. Computerized crime reports and file searching will increase surveilance efficiency. Computers have been used by educators for several years, and this use will continue to expand. Computer-assisted instruction will be used from elementary schools through graduate schools, and computers will also facilitate testing and research in most learning environments. In homes computers will assist in cooking, operating appliances, shopping, record keeping, and so forth. Modern medicine will use computers in hospital drug inventories,

the contributions of idea people

patient monitoring, patient treatment, medical research, and other related areas. Athletic events, urban transportation systems, and industries of most types will be computer assisted in their operations. Few areas of our urbanized society will escape the impact of computers.[24]

Cybernetics is another recent development of the knowledge explosion. The original basis of cybernetics was developed in 1948, primarily through the work of Norbert Wiener at the Massachusetts Institute of Technology. Defined as the science of control and communication in the animal and the machine, it is in fact an outgrowth of engineering research during World War II. The field of cybernetics is expanding, and as concern with systems grows in importance, the science of cybernetics will possibly cause another revolution in American society.[25] In any event as society becomes more systematic in its social organization, computers and cybernation hold at least the possibility of a higher quality of human environment.

welfare and birth control

The Great Depression dealt a severe psychological blow to the dreams of the American middle class. The social welfare schemes of the New Deal, a product of the Depression and the thirties, were designed by specialists from a variety of disciplines. These programs were designed to rebuild people's faith in themselves and to restore their ability to compete successfully. By the late 1950s and early 1960s, it had become unmistakably apparent that pockets of poverty existed and were not being eradicated by the increasing size and the increasing costs of the welfare programs. The ideology of a free and competitive society did not square well with increasingly expensive welfare programs, especially ones that did not work. Moreover, it was clear that poverty was being intensively concentrated in the core areas of large cities while the white and affluent middle classes were moving to suburban areas where industrial parks were providing the better types of employment opportunities.

President Johnson's War on Poverty, which became a focus of ideas, programs, and money during the 1960s, was profoundly influenced by the intellectual community. Most specifically Michael Harrington's book *The Other America* (1962) was a major factor in focusing concern and motivating action.[26] Harrington argued that society's own organization was generating subcultures of poverty within society. Richard Cloward and Lloyd Ohlin, in their book *Delinquency and Opportunity*, further challenged the social welfare establishment. They argued that deficiencies in the environment and in job opportunities rather than in individuals were the primary causes of delinquency and poverty.

Out of this new focusing on the organization of society more than on the individual, the leaders in this reform movement, called the "Young Turks," in social welfare developed programs like Mobilization For Youth, The Office of Economic Opportunity, Head Start, and many others. Like so many other idea contributions, the results have been difficult to measure. New configurations in society have clearly developed, but their effect is questionable. In the short run there is little record of achievement. Nevertheless, the power of idea people to shift and change social structures is clearly illustrated in these programs.

Changes in the social welfare system continue. Powerful new ideas that would provide child day-care centers on a extensive basis, guaranteed income, along with additional housing and health facilities are being proposed. These types of changes move the planned society forward in the face of an ever-weakening free enterprise ideology.

Eugenics is receiving a larger and larger audience as concerns for family planning, birth control, sterilization, artificial insemination, and euthanasia increase. While there are few concepts that will arouse greater prejudice than eugenics, specific views of societal modification are becoming accepted.[27] Careful and detailed studies of the biology of reproduction continue to be conducted. While much of this research is devoted to family planning and birth control, the

the contributions of idea people

basic research in these areas also provides more insight for selectionist eugenics, transformationist eugenics, biological engineering, and more information for sperm banks and artificial insemination.

In the face of threatening global overpopulation, religious and moral support for family planning, birth control, sterilization, euthanasia, and so on is increasing. At the very minimum all of these subjects are increasingly matters of societal concern. This is combined with *Futurist* articles suggesting new patterns of family organization. It would be normative for many married couples to have no children and for others to have a large number of children, six to eight, far above the current family size. For families with a larger number of children, child rearing would be the primary occupation of the husband and wife.[28] Researchers have also continued work in the area of population and birth control. They engage in extensive research, publish books and journals, organize symposiums, and participate in developing national population policies ranging from birth control to abortion. Their work has produced a variety of studies including "Cybernetics of Population Control," "Biology of Fertility Controls in Underdeveloped Areas," "Frontiers in Methods of Fertility Control," "Some Facts about Legal Abortion," and "Socio-Cultural Aspects of Population Growth."[29] The technology of contributions in these areas is continually held back by concerns for invasion of privacy and by traditional moral values.

The many advances in medicine in the twentieth century have often been spectacular. Organ transplants are among the most dramatic of these accomplishments. The first successful heart transplant was in 1967 in Cape Town, South Africa. The second one was successfully performed a year later.[30] These high points of achievement do not solve the major problems of heart disease, but they illustrate innovative directions in medicine. The ability to perform kidney transplants is even more developed. Research to make kidney transplanting possible was systematically started in 1946.[31] By the middle of the twentieth century physicians had little possibility of doing more than repairing or removing a damaged or diseased organ. In the near future it is probable that there will be widespread transplanting of kidneys, lungs, hearts, stomachs, intestines, and other organs. The possibility of replacement with either another human organ or a mechanical organ made by engineers is increasingly real. Artificial hearts, kidneys, lungs etc. are being developed and improved.[32]

Even more important than artificial organs, which are designed to be used permanently, are life-preserving machines, like heart boosters and heart pacemakers. These machines may assist a person through a critical period and allow a diseased or damaged organ to recover. This type of care also avoids some of the critical ethical problems faced with transplants of other human organs and the long-term use of artificial organs. In the near future physicians will be able to use automated machines for laboratory testing and analysis, the results of which will be shown on computer printouts. This kind of hardware will help distinguish abnormal conditions and speed diagnosis and treatment by cross-tabulations with other patient characteristics.

The problems and practice of medicine are the result of dramatic advances in medical science in the twentieth century. Advances in medicine are so extensive that phrases like "miracle drugs" are now commonplace. Research has been conducted in virtually every possible area of study. Researchers now study both birth-control and death-control devices. New processes and new mechanical devices continue to be improved, and new research information provides increasingly sophisticated techniques.

communication

The technology of communication has been revolutionized in the past quarter of a century. It has been an interdisciplinary and a multidisciplinary effort involving engineers, linguists, biologists, neurologists, psychologists, and sociologists, In the world of ideas it is always difficult to date the starting point

the contributions of idea people

for a new notion, yet historians and others attempt the task. One of the most important thrusts came in 1948 when Claude Shannon of Bell Laboratories published *Communication Theory*. Like most advances in communications, this new theory rested heavily on the pure mathematical research of persons like Norbert Wiener.[33]

It was also in the 1950s that television as a specific communication technology emerged as a major force on society —a position it continues to hold.[34] The impact of television can be seen in the ways it has modified life from preschool Sesame Street education to political campaigning. Television levels culture and brings a common knowledge of men and events from everywhere to everywhere—to virtually all people regardless of socioeconomic class. The impact of this technology is illustrated by a few examples. On the evening of March 7, 1955, one out of every two Americans watched Mary Martin play in *Peter Pan* on television. Never before had a single person had so large an audience.[35] The so-called "Great Debate" in 1960 between Kennedy and Nixon changed campaigning for the American presidency.[36] The full impact of televising the bloody horrors of war or sporting events or symphonic concerts in technicolor to homes throughout the nation requires further study to be more fully understood.

Nevertheless, even developments in telecommunications continue unabated. For example the development of Tel Star in the 1960s relays direct television communication around the world. It was accepted so quickly that it now appears to have been with us for a long time.[37]

There is little doubt that a government's needs and positions can be strongly expressed when presidents, governors, mayors, and other important leaders speak to their constituents in face-to-face—but one-way dialogues. The institution of democracy is necessarily modified. While the nature and direction of this modification continues to be worked out, there are groups meeting, like the Fair Campaigning Practices Committee which first convened in 1965, to confer about the problem of television in politics.[38] The Federal

Communications Commission addresses itself to questions concerning the impact of television as a central element in American life. Questions of fairness and the high cost of television have become almost perennial. Two major norms have been promulgated in an effort to bring some order in the social impact of television on the American life style. These norms are stated in Section 315 of the Federal Communications Act and in the Fairness Doctrine. First, all legally qualified candidates for public office during campaign seasons are to be extended equal opportunity. In practice, this rule is operative for perhaps the six months preceding election day in every even-numbered year for candidates for the U.S. Congress and for about ten months every four years for candidates for the presidency. The second Fairness Doctrine norm applies to ideas as well as to personalities. Hearings must be granted to all sides. Individuals and their ideas which have been subject to attack must be allowed an opportunity to express their point of view.[39]

The high cost of political campaigning by television continues to be an important national issue. In 1964 it was estimated that $35 million was paid by candidates for broadcasts on radio and television and approximately $200 million was the cost of television for political activities of all levels of government.[40] While efforts have been made to limit the amount which might be expended on this type of political campaigning, no adequate solutions yet have been reached. The problem continues to be a major issue.

Still other societal manifestations of the impact of mass communications are reflected in movements like the one begun by Marshal McLuhan.[41] McLuhan's rise was sudden and substantial. By his dictum, "the medium is the massage," he became in effect the high priest of "Pop" advertising. A more full statement of his position was developed in *Understanding Media*, which became a national best seller. He saw television as the "cool medium." Prior to the innovation of the mass media, the dramatic impact of "great debates" and "cool media" were inconceivable.

the contributions of idea people

Television, radio, along with the mass production and distribution of newspapers, magazines, motion pictures, paper back books, and other printed matter constitute major elements of an urbanized society. Although some people may experience alienation in the middle of a large crowd, few persons in the urbanized society have any real opportunity to escape the oppressiveness of the herd and live a hermit's life. The communications media bring the society together in ways that are yet to be fully understood.[42]

technological contributions

The hallmark of American innovation is technology. It has made America famous and, more recently among a vocal minority, infamous. Among the most dramatic of the technological leaps are those achieved in space. Russia's 1957 Sputnik was a challenge to American technology, pride, and world prestige. One of the greatest technological races in history was launched. Almost at once Congress passed the National Aeronautics and Space Act (NASA). More scientists, engineers, and other creative thinkers than ever before in any one project were recruited. NASA developed a ten-year plan, culminating in the manned lunar landings of 1969. A $20 to $40 billion investment in personnel and materials facilitated the development of Apollo and put men on the moon.[43] Scientists continue to study the materials and facts obtained from the lunar missions. Although many aspects of the space program are winding down, advances continue.

The range of technological contributions is enormous. A few of the products developed by just one company, Arthur D. Little, is astonishing. In the 1950s an Arthur D. Little chemical-engineering team led by Julian Avery made the first improvement on the blast furnace since 1895—the pressure top. It was first used commercially by Republic Steel.[44] Development of the "jet tapper," used on the open hearth blast furnace, was also led by an Arthur D. Little research team, this one headed by Doctor Bruce Old. The device combines the various shaped charges used in the bazooka and applied in industrial safe cracking. Through a $16,000 research project, the jet tapper was produced and ultimately marketed by the DuPont Company.[45]

Little's accomplishments are not limited to the steel industry. It has been a leader in research throughout the twentieth century.

In the first quarter of the twentieth century, the Arthur D. Little firm was retained by Owen-Illinois Glass to help standardize and cut costs in that industry. It was discovered that the viscosity range of glass must be controlled. To do so the viscosimeter was developed. Its use has cut costs and reduced formulas and contributed directly and greatly to more business profit.[46]

In the mid-1930s Arthur D. Little was asked by the U.S. Navy to develop potable water in large quantities from sea water for use in submarine fleets. Under the leadership of Dr. Robert Kleinschmidt, a physicist and mechanical engineer, they produced what was known as the Kleinschmidt still. This contribution doubled the cruising range of the U.S. submarine fleet during World War II, when $100 million worth of the stills were installed.[47]

Bristol-Myers' brush-making subsidiary, called Rubberset, engaged the Arthur D. Little firm in the 1950s to assist in developing a substitute for the hog bristles which had previously been obtained from China. The product developed was a cheap source of keratin, the major protein component of bristle. The new source was found in chicken feathers.[48]

Other contributions are less convincing—indeed conjectural. Cloud seeding is a case in point. For a number of years now, there have been requests from agriculturalists for assistance in water production by rain making. Government and university meteorologists have been reluctant to engage extensively in this work, and in their absence commercial firms have proceeded, even in the face of considerable uncertainty. Some successes are notable and, indeed, cloud seeders submit that precipitation can usually be increased between 20 to 40 percent.[49] The cloud-seeding operation has become a multi-million dollar business and continues to grow. Firms are located in the Mountain States, the Far West, and the North East. Hard questions are associated with the rain-making industry in terms of liability for flooding and damage and, to date, these kinds of questions remain unsolved.

In America some of the most notable new ideas have been developed in food and fiber production. The U.S. Department of Agriculture researchers, agricultural experiment station researchers at universities, and private industry have combined efforts to build new production machinery and to use chemicals in production and quality control. Accordingly a sharply declining number of food-and fiber-producing workers provide an increasing and high quality-controlled product.[50] Scientists in agriculture also work on a worldwide basis. There are probably no areas where their contributions have contributed more directly to the welfare of man than in food production. Rice and wheat developments in the Philippines, India, and Latin America provide new hope for millions of people by increasing both the quantity and quality of agricultural output. Aggressive and imaginative research is being done to provide long-time preservation of foods through ionizing radiation. Work is being done to expand hydroponic techniques of production. In world food production scientists have achieved notable accomplishments.

Among the most spectacular contributions of scientists have been the peaceful uses of atomic power. In August 1955 sixty nations convened in Geneva, Switzerland, the International Conference on Peaceful Uses of Atomic Energy. The results were favorably impressive and held out a new hope for higher human quality of existence than ever before had been imagined.[51] The Atomic Energy Commission in the United States has become a major force in this new direction. In addition some one thousand companies have "hot labs" and several hundred are regular customers of the Atomic Energy Commission's radioisotopes. New atomic uses include radiation's influence on chemical reactions for keeping potatoes

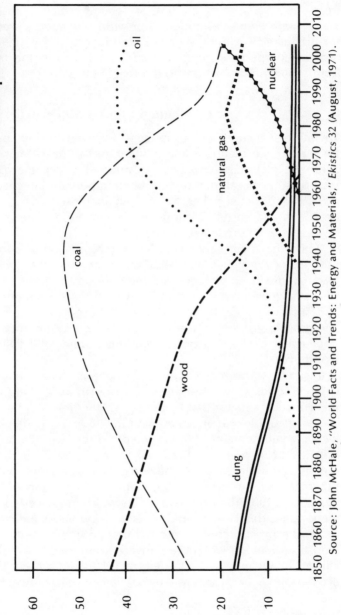

figure 7.1
world consumption of fuels

Source: John McHale, "World Facts and Trends: Energy and Materials," *Ekistics* 32 (August, 1971).

from spoiling, altering plastics, et cetera.[52] Nuclear-powered reactors are being developed to provide new energy required for urbanized societies. A major world hope is for increased nuclear energy consumption. Figure 7.1 indicates the trends from 1950 with projections to the year 2000.[53]

new contributions: the revolution in life styles

Technological contributions range widely. They include peaceful uses of war materials and military uses of peace materials. Synthetic materials have been developed to replace natural materials, physical nature has been modified by chemical processes, food supplies have been increased by scientific breeding, and so on. Technological innovation is one of the hallmarks of an urbanized society.

While the most general understanding of contributions is in terms of the tangible material things or specific techniques associated with them, contemporary notions and ideas themselves have become important as contributions. Ecumenopolis is a sufficiently complex example of the power of an idea. The diffusion of this concept has made a profound impact on intellectual circles and on real-life environmental quality the world over.

In simple terms the concept ecumenopolis means universal or continuous city.[54] The projections of urban growth, using this concept, suggest that by the year 2000 there will be some 163 megalopolises, contrasted with the 18 in 1971, which collectively will contain 45 to 50 percent of the world's population. By 2050 megalopolises will be replaced by urbanized regions. Between 2070 and the end of the twenty-first century, urbanized regions in turn will be replaced by urbanized continents. By 2100 urbanized continents will be replaced by ecumenopolis. This later condition, ecumenopolis, is anticipated to be the most highly developed unit of human settlement. Man's settlement will have moved from mere agricultural villages in ancient times through the urbanized present to the ecumenopolis of the future—by only a few years hence.[55]

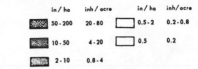

figure 7.2
ecumenopolis in the United States (study by ACE, 1968)

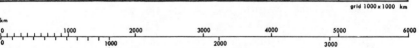

Source: C. A. Doxiadis, "Man's Movement and His Settlements," *Ekistics* 29 (May, 1970).

figure 7.3
ecumenopolis in the world, 2060 (study by ACE, revised 1969)

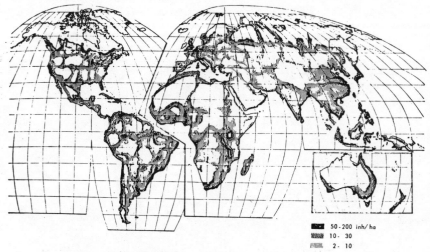

50 - 200 inh/ ha
10 - 30
2 - 10

Source: C. A. Doxiadis, "Man's Movement and His Settlements," Ekistics 29 (May, 1970).

The concept of ecumenopolis and supporting data suggest that the world population in the next 100 to 150 years will be in the range of 15 to 25 billion—in contrast to the more than 3 billion in 1970 and the anticipated 6 billion by 2000. Major questions are being raised and much research is being conducted concerning the amount of water and energy sufficient to sustain this kind of dense urban population. This concept of life in the future anticipates that illiteracy will be virtually eradicated prior to the full advent of the age of ecumenopolis. It also anticipates that high levels of nutrition and health, approximately equal to that in advanced countries in the latter part of the twentieth century, will be achieved on a worldwide basis during the first half of the twenty-first century. Once this level of human development has been achieved, it will probably be sustained for many centuries.[56] Figures 7.2 and

7.3 show the projected developing map for this new world and for the United States during the same period.[57]

idea diffusion

Ideas are challenged, if not plagued, by the relatively limited cost of basic research and the generally much higher cost of applied research and development. It is reported, for example, that the basic research which produced penicillin perhaps did not cost more than $20,000, but it cost millions to get penicillin into mass production.[58]

Many studies of the diffusion of technological innovation have been made in recent years. The ultimate impact of contributions depends on the process and rate of diffusion. National Science Foundation researchers in studying this situation suggested that the following influence rates of idea acceptance:

1. As the number of firms and industries adopting an innovation increases, the probability of its adoption by a nonuser increases.
2. The expected profitability of an innovation influences the probability of its adoption.
3. For equally profitable innovations, the probability of adoption tends to be slower for innovation requiring relatively large investments.
4. The probability of adoption of an innovation is dependent on the industry in which the innovation is introduced.[59]

NSF studies also indicated that, when new ideas require the replacement of still usable physical equipment, the rate of introduction is reduced. If an innovation can be adopted in a firm that is rapidly expanding the probability of diffusion will be quickened.

The conclusion of the National Science Foundation investigation is that diffusion typically is a slow process. In most cases a decade or more is involved for major firms to partici-

the contributions of idea people

pate in the introduction and use of the new idea. As the profitability is increased, the rate of diffusion is accordingly increased.

summary—implications

The contributions of creative thinkers, from the most esoteric
basic research through applied research and development
and to creative administrative innovation, all reflect the nature
of their profession. In this chapter we examined a few contributions to understand the nature of creative work and not
simply to enumerate contributions as such. This chapter is a
final phase of the study of idea people and is a preparation
for the analysis of policy implications considered in Chapter
Eight. The way creative people formulate their ideas and
render them in concrete material forms and in social organizational forms is influenced by their manpower characteristics,
and those in turn are influenced by their training environment.

The purpose of this book is to stimulate the development
of an optimum manpower-training policy for idea people. A
precarious balance of such an optimum environment is difficult precisely because of the diffusive nature of contributions
generated and the diffuse needs of society. Our society faces
hard questions concerning the development of training and
manpower policies in a world so characterized by innovation,
plurality, and variability. While that is difficult, and there is a
tendency to avoid facing up to such difficult situations, the
avoidance is more serious—leaving possible, if not probable,
greater amounts of frustration and lower amounts of productivity by creative people for society. A manpower-training
policy must be an overt integral part of society. It must provide
for and even encourage a full range of contribution. It must
be a mainstay of the creative environment.

I dea people constitute a major part of America's labor force. As professionals and managers they total about 25 percent of the nation's labor force, but they in effect control the remaining three-fourths. On the one hand, idea people have been elevated to the level of an elite class in American society, yet from another point of view, these otherwise illustrious and powerful people are obscure, classless, and ordinary citizens. Indeed some idea people suggest that they are given too little recognition and are anything but a power elite. Regardless of how one views the status of idea people, they must be carefully dealt with because our ubanized, post-industrial, and cybernating society depends on them.

For all practical purposes idea people are new as a major component in American society. Their massive arrival is a phenomenon of the second half of the twentieth century. Idea people came into existence to fill major needs when America was industrializing and urbanizing. They are products of the society and at the same time major molders of the society's being and its new directions.

The origins of creative people indicate that they are mavericks, intelligent and individualistic. In most cases, through personal discipline, they achieve mastery of their professions after long periods of university training. Due to the complex nature of their professions, many sacrifice a life of ease for

8

policy implications – manpower planning and training coordination

a life of frustration—of intellectual and social stress. The training of idea people is both long and expensive. Moreover with an accelerating rate of knowledge proliferation their training is evermore a continuous life-long process. The knowledge which most will need to have in the latter part of their productive life is not yet discovered when they enter universities. Therefore, society must organize both training and employment so that regular long and short periods of retraining are typically part of the idea person's career.

The United States government and its laissez-faire system of universities were both organized prior to the advent of large numbers of idea people. Neither the structure of government nor the organization of universities anticipated or provided for the demanding roles which idea people would carry out in the last of the twentieth century. External forces seem to have provided major thrusts for moving American society to fully accommodate creative people. Needs created by World War II and the challenge of the Russian sputnik accelerated both the training and use of idea people. By the 1970s both training and use of idea people have extended far beyond defense and space.

The nation has followed more a series of "crash programs" than a systematic policy in encouraging people to commit themselves to idea careers and in providing research, development, and utilization support for specific idea work. Since the federal government is both the major supporter and user of defense and aerospace research, it has, even on an ad hoc basis, been able to provide considerable direction. The free enterprise society prides itself on giving its citizens opportunities for career choices, but it disavows responsibility when its changes in priorities create widespread career frustration and unemployment. Many idea people obtained training for specific areas in science by government stipends designed to quickly move people into defense and space careers. With military hardware and space program contract cancellations, many of the nation's highly trained scientists and engineers have had to seek alternate employment and obtain retraining or experience personal anxiety combined with unemployment. Such shifts in national priorities and in occupational needs are devastating to individual morale and costly to the national economy. The Emergency Employment Act in the 1970s was in part related to severe unemployment experienced by engineers and other highly trained aerospace manpower.

Now the nation faces a major expansion of knowledge beyond the Department of Defense, Atomic Energy Commission, and the National Aeronautics and Space Administration. Advances in the federal departments of Health, Education and Welfare, Agriculture, Interior, Transportation, Commerce, and Housing and Urban Development are needed.[1] The amount of money spent on research projects indicates the direction of knowledge development. The federal government will continue to make the largest dollar contribution to the support, training, and use of professionals. In 1972 it is estimated that some $30 billion funded the nation's research and development work. Of this total nearly $16 billion was provided by the federal government. In contrast, in 1962 the nation's research and development funding totaled nearly $16 billion, of which nearly $10 billion was provided by the federal government.[2]

Considering the number of creative people, the cost of their training, the amount of their salaries, and the cost of research and development, the magnitude of this part of the nation's labor force is massive. The need for their expertise in contemporary America and the idealogical stance of the democratic society, which favors the individual's freedom of occupational choice, clearly signify the importance of an idea people manpower-planning policy. Furthermore, a manpower-planning policy should assist universities in organizing their training to serve individuals and assist the schools in maximizing productivity from scarce educational dollars. Both individuals and society need more assurance that full and stimulating careers rather than unemployment will be the fruitful reward of training and work.

idea people and societal interdependence

Idea people and the urbanized American society have grown to be greatly dependent on each other. This interdependency has come about rapidly and with little plan. When Mr. Eisenhower was president, he was concerned that the nation's public policy might become the captive of a scientific-technological elite.[3] The Eisenhower administration was so concerned about the science-technology power growth that it attempted to cut federal spending in this area, but it failed. During that administration research and development budgets quadrupled. The additional congressional appropriations were for far more than defense. For example, the National Institutes of Health obtained a nine-fold increase during the period of the Eisenhower administration.

There is continuing concern that the scientific revolution and specially trained scientists are upsetting the historic system of governmental checks and balances. Although the American constitution was established during the Age of Enlightenment, it preceded the era of science and professional people. Even the word scientist was not used at the time the government was established. Science as a method of inquiry was then in its infancy.[4]

As early as the mid-1930s, there was recognition of and use of specialists. President Roosevelt set up a science advisory board staffed by specialists to help combat the Great Depression by designing numerous public works programs. With the advent of the World War II, professionals increased their role in contributing to government needs and often exercised a great deal of initiative and independence in advising the government. Frequently they carried on research specifically for the government, but this work often went beyond governmental service to work for universities and industry but on problems clearly related to government needs.[5]

The interrelation of idea people and society is particularly confounding to nations like America. When pushed to the ultimate, creative people are neither democratic nor responsible to a nation as such. This is not to imply disloyalty—in fact the opposite may be true. But ideas know no loyalty and idea people have often been troubled when their knowledge has been exploited beyond their own national boundaries. Nevertheless, as ideas become a dominant force in the world's urbanized societies and as creative people are utilized increasingly by private industries, many industrial firms will become supra-national—some already have moved in this direction.[6] Therefore governments like the United States increasingly create and expand agencies to integrate specialists into their structure. In 1962 the Office of Science Technology was created and made a part of the executive office of the president.[7]

With the growth of idea people, and their societal interdependency, calls for the establishment of a federal department of science increase.[8] Such a department would be intended to increase the operating effectiveness of government programs in science and engineering. The department would also be expected to increase efficiency, provide higher status for research, introduce sound policy development, and so forth. Indeed it would be designed to have direct influence over, if not control of, a wide range of programs involving specialists and their research for the Department of Defense, Atomic Energy Commission, National Science Foundation, National Aeronautics and Space Administration, the Department of Health, Education and Welfare, the Department of Agriculture, the Department of Housing and Urban Development, Department of Transportation, and other departments involving major research programs. Many times in the past, and extending to the present, opposition has exceeded support for a federal science department. Nevertheless, the problematic situation this position recognizes is germane to manpower needs.

With increasing frequency idea people have addressed themselves to questions concerning the knowledge explosion and the maintenance of free societies in which decisions are made on the basis of systematic knowledge. While their views of what is the proper relationship vary, idea people have exercised the most forthright leadership in bringing their ideas to serve what in their judgment is the interest of the nation and the world.[9] For example, the dangers may be expressed as follows: "Either knowledge will be so accumulative as to dishearten men, or the control of knowledge will come into the hands of an elite, who may employ the power of knowledge for purposes contrary to the democratic belief in role and judgment."[10] Other dimensions of the problem of the interdependency of ideas, creative people, and urbanized society are found in publications like the *Scientific Estate*[11] and the *New Utopians*.[12] In these monographs questions concerning the adjustments which political institutions must make in relation to the scientific revolution and the purposes which technology will serve are raised. In the *Scientific Estate* it is argued that although idea production is crucial to political affairs, little or no theory concerning the proper role of each has been developed. Idea people are moving the public and private sectors closer together. In doing this a new order of complexity is introduced into the governmental management of the society. A collection of factors from .automation, computers, systems engineering, operations research, and cybernetics are all contributing to the reorganization of society. The role of political expediency and individual free choice in this revolutionary reorganization of society is unclear.

When John F. Kennedy was president he said, concerning this situation, that men of science should set their research purposes, and society, in supporting science, must put forth its own needs.[13] The assertion is clear. Carrying it out is the matter of question—a matter for which no appropriate technique has yet been developed. Toward this end, some suggest three policy components. The first of these is "science in policy." This approach would describe the roles of idea people in using the knowledge base to analyze programs and proposals on their technical merits. The second is "policy

in science." This concerns societal support for creative inquiry. The third element is "scientists for policy." In this
situation the concern is for the use of scientists and other
idea people as resources in policy making itself.[14] Jerome
Wiesner, when director of the Office of Science and Technology, indicated that one of the greatest problems facing
America was the determination of objectives for science
and technology in serving the entire society and the obtaining of appropriate support both from the Congress and the
executive branch of government. Secondly, he indicated that
America must utilize more energy and develop better administrative tools for making and implementing decisions related
to science and technology. The third problem to which he
called specific attention was the need for better techniques
of communication between and among specialists themselves
and between specialists and the general population of which
they are a part.[15]

Some of the special problems concerning the labyrinth of
interrelations between idea people and the Congress exist
because most congressmen have a general background in
law or business and lack the training that would facilitate
their understanding of scientists. Typically Congress uses
committees and subcommittees to study various issues. These
committees hold hearings and invite individuals, many of
whom are technical scientists, to testify as expert witnesses.
Appearances recently have been made by radiologists, genet-
icists, pathologists, biochemists, meteorologists, physicists,
and many others. Often these technical experts have added,
in effect, more confusion than elucidation. Panels of experts
are used in some cases, but their findings are different more
by degree than by kind from the committee hearings.[16]

Congress is itself concerned about its apparent increasing
inability to understand, lead, or even oversee specialized programs. Part of this congressional concern relates to the cost
of research and development, which for the federal government alone has increased from nearly $10 billion in 1962 to

almost $16 billion in 1972. In addition to the budget itself, many congressional leaders are concerned about their general lack of ability to oversee the effective use of the government's money in these areas. Thirdly, many congressional leaders are apprehensive about their ability to give leadership to "big science" so that it will beneficially serve the entire nation.[17]

A final illustration of the interdependency between society and idea people is shown by the George B. Pegram Lectureships at the Brookhaven National Laboratory. This new lecture series was established specifically to cultivate interaction between science and the other aspects of society. The lectureships are provided to give a scholar several weeks to reside at the laboratory and to have both formal and informal contact with the staff. The series itself is named in honor of one of America's great scientists, a professor of physics, who was dean and vice-president of Columbia University and who assisted the government in using nuclear energy for the nation's defense. Pegram himself was instrumental in the founding of the Brookhaven National Laboratory.[18]

An increasing proportion of Americans recognize the interdependence of idea people and the urbanized society. Few question the validity of this interdependence. Most who are knowledgeable concerning the situation, however, see the need for an appropriate balance in the partnership and are seeking ways to achieve it. This monograph, accordingly, seeks to further focus the need for manpower policy and planning at the highest level for a free society, and for individual career satisfaction. It also identifies and specifies in some detail the need for coordinating university training of idea people. This coordination is needed both to serve individuals as they exercise free training choices, and to serve the large number of independent universities in obtaining and making wise use of resources. It also is intended to serve governments, industries, and private citizens as they seek to appropriate adequate funding for the high cost of training and retraining idea people.

Currently America has no manpower policy for idea people, or more specifically no policy for professionals and executives. The U.S. Department of Labor has no office which is charged with specifically addressing itself to matters of idea people manpower policy, although such an office has been recommended by the National Manpower Advisory Committee. The National Science Foundation produces statistics concerning the current number of scientists and professionals with some reasonable regularity. These data specify their places of employment and to some extent their work characteristics, income, and training experiences. Between 1960 and 1970 professionals, as a major component of the idea people manpower, were the most rapidly growing occupational category in the nation. From 1970 to 1980 the U.S. Department of Labor expects professionals to continue as the most rapidly growing single occupational category, even though the anticipated rate of increase will be less than the preceding decade.[19]

The current census enumerations of idea people appear reasonably satisfactory for the nation. Enumerations for states and local labor market areas, however, are generally deficient or nonexistent. The problem is a difficult one because idea people are among the most mobile individuals in America. There is even less information concerning the proportion of idea people who are privately and publicly employed. Many idea people are able to shift from one specific area of work to another on a reasonably short time span. Consequently, in local labor market areas the quality of data describing the work and other characteristics of idea people is extremely weak.

Forecasting needs—surpluses and shortages—of idea people is precarious. Such projections are of dubious quality at the national level and generally of less quality as one moves to local labor markets. Accordingly it is difficult for potential employers to identify their manpower pools. It is difficult for idea people to survey the universe of opportunities for their own careers and to become acquainted with the needs for their services nationally or locally. Most of all it is a nearly impossible task for university training centers to be "on target" in preparing an appropriate number of idea people when systematic counts of current practitioners and projections are so few and so doubtful.[20]

The gross absence of manpower policy for specialists in a free enterprise society is unsatisfactory and abusive. In such a critical manpower area, where the content of work itself is difficult and demanding, individuals who seek to achieve for themselves and to serve society ought not to be faced with so much frustration and unemployment due to lack of manpower policy and planning. Also, American society faces a high probability of continual swing from crisis to crisis and from emergency to emergency while there is an absence of systematic planning and projecting for idea manpower. The federal government is the largest single employer of idea people. A few other large corporations like American Telephone and Telegraph Company, General Motors, General Electric, United States Steel, Great Atlantic and Pacific Tea Company, and the state governments are other major employers. Planning needs to start with a careful and continual description of the work done and the characteristics of idea people in the major employing areas. In 1967 the Bureau of Labor Statistics did a specific piece of research to ascertain some of the characteristics of scientists and engineers employed by state governments. Only 3 percent of the idea people were employed in state governments at that time. The categories used were scientists, engineers, health and related professionals, social workers, and technicians. Their places of work were differentiated into health and welfare agencies, highway and public work agencies, agriculture and conservation agencies, and other agencies. The study shows a rapid rate of growth for these kinds of personnel in state governments between 1964 and 1967. However, no projections are regularly made for their future needs.[21] In 1970 the

Bureau of Labor Statistics published the results of a study of scientists and engineers working in private industry. The bureau projected the needs for such personnel through 1980. The study showed a total of 35,800 employed in 1968 and a projected need for 55,000 or a 53.5 percent increase by 1980. Details were specified for engineers, mathematicians, physical scientists, and life scientists.[22]

mobility

Manpower policy concerning idea people must recognize mobility both as an advantage in shifting their focus and ability and as a liability for projecting the number of persons needed in various jobs. To a considerable extent, society moves idea people by viewing them as an investment, which from one point of view they are.[23] Even internationally there is a "brain drain." Somewhat similar to society's moving idea people as investments, idea people move themselves in directions of opportunities to research, study, and innovate in areas of greatest interest to them. Therefore they can be quickly moved to a company, agency, or university which will offer the machines, equipment, or other resources which will facilitate their idea interest most at a particular point in their career. Or they will move to a location which has a so-called "critical mass" of persons who are or can become a stimulating body of colleagues for their particular inquiry interest.

Probably the most fluid characteristic of idea people mobility is their capacity to shift with intellectual agility from one area of inquiry, research, or expertise to another. Moreover it is idea people themselves who make new areas of inquiry. They create areas like cybernation, aerospace, organ transplants, and so forth. They develop training opportunities so that selected idea people can quickly move into the new areas.

manpower model—traditional

Traditionally a manpower model was developed implicitly and without specific plans. That implicit model was to train idea people for the first twenty to twenty-five years of life (see Figure 8.1). After the training, it was expected that they

figure 8.1.
traditionally implied manpower model

age 25	age 65	age 72
TRAIN about 4 to 8 years	*WORK* about 40 to 45 years	*RETIRE* about 10 to 15 years

should work, serving themselves and society for the next forty to forty-five years. The final phase in this model is retirement for ten to fifteen years. The implicit assumption in the model is that we know enough about idea production and work needs forty to forty-five years in advance so that we can train people in their upper teens and early twenties for a work life expectancy of forty to forty-five years. This means that in the 1970s we, according to this model, ought to be preparing people in the universities for a work life into the second decade of the twenty-first century. But from the middle of this century to the present, it has become increasingly clear that the body of knowledge which many idea people will be using in the last half of their forty to forty-five year career is not even known in the first half of their work career—much less is it available at the time of their training.

manpower model—new

As a post-industrial American society critically examines its idea people needs and opportunities, a new manpower model is needed. One direction for illustrating such a new model is as follows (see Figure 8.2). It implies a reasonably clear distinction between occupational training and education for its own sake. The emphasis is disproportionately on occupational training from about age twenty to thirty and disproportionately on general education from ages thirty to fifty. The most significant departure from the traditional model is the continual training and education from about age twenty

figure 8.2
possible new manpower model

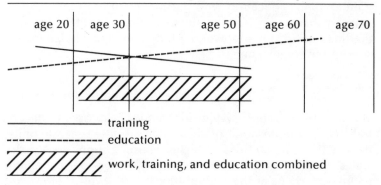

age 20 | age 30 | age 50 | age 60 | age 70

——————— training

- - - - - - - - - - - education

///////// work, training, and education combined

through about age seventy. Work will proceed from about age twenty or twenty-five through age sixty. Also from age twenty to twenty-five through about age fifty, training will regularly be intermixed with work. Depending on the nature of one's idea work, the technical training should proceed for one or two days a week, one week a month, one month a year, or a sabbatical year following every third or fourth year of work. From about age thirty through age seventy, training and education will proceed at approximately equal proportions. With the shorter work week there will be appropriate time available to expand both training and education. A large amount of the training may well be conducted by professors in the work environment of agency or industrial laboratories. The typical college student, particularly for general education, will be age thirty and over. From about age fifty on to age seventy, training will be virtually eliminated and replaced with education. Idea people will in effect shift the imaginative focus of their intellects from occupational work to educational explorations.

This new model anticipates the dominance of idea power in the society of the future. It seeks to achieve continual life-long dignity for individuals with extensive intellectual acumen. It anticipates the character of creative work involving the need for maximum mobility and shifting. Both continual training and education will facilitate shifting this critical mass of manpower and, at the same time, facilitate keeping that mass of idea manpower alerted to the knowledge explosion and to societal needs.

university training coordination

The higher education system in America is massively decentralized. From one point of view there are fifty separate units, namely those institutions of higher learning supported by the states. These institutions enroll nearly three-fourths of the nation's students at the higher educational levels.[24] However, at the doctoral training level, some sixty or seventy of the nation's universities produce between 70 and 80 percent of all graduate school doctoral degrees. Almost half of these schools are private.[25]

Even within the state-supported units of higher education there is considerable diversity. Most of the state-supported schools make some contribution to the training of idea people. Often within the fifty states there is vigorous competition between and among so-called state college systems and state university systems. Even as many of the state universities expand to multiple campuses there continues to be competition among the several units of a single university. The proportion of the nation's population continuing to post-secondary education is still increasing. Consequently, the cost of financing higher education accelerates. Indeed it is one of the most expensive items in state government in the so-called non-dedicated expenditure area. And while the federal and private contributions to higher education are a small part of the total cost, both of these sources of funding in effect give direction to manpower at the highest levels. The federal government contributes significantly to stipends for graduate training and to facilities for instruction. The big private universities are among the leaders in doctoral-level training.

In recent years coordinating boards for higher education are being established and expanded in the fifty states. Some professional associations are making systematic surveys of the supply and demand of practitioners in their areas. In England there is increasing demand for responsible planning for post-graduate scientific education, as there has been for medical education.[26] The coordinating boards note the call for planning of higher education needs are not withdrawals from implicit policy notions that competition in ideas and in training of idea people is an important mechanism for excellence. It does, however, suggest that both individual satisfaction and societal needs and resources will be more adequately served by regular and continual systematic analysis of supply and demand. Indeed, Ableson of the American Association for the Advancement of Science is among those who suggest that in the absence of planning the almost ad hoc decisions of government to expand stipends and resources in one area and contract them in another in a reasonably short span of years constitutes, in fact, a type of negative meddling in higher education on the part of the federal government.[27]

Near chaos and contradiction characterize the head counts and projections of high talent manpower at the doctoral level. It is difficult to get even satisfactory comparative data on doctoral personnel in the nation because of the almost random inclusion and exclusion of Ph.D.s, doctorates in education and range of professional doctorates.

One of the most comprehensive counts and projections of doctoral-level production in the United States is shown in Table 8.1. The range of doctoral degrees awarded in 1971 extends from 27,000 to nearly 33,000. The anticipated production by 1980 ranges from 45,000 to 78,000. By the year 2000 the production range is from 72,000 to 120,000. The Council of Graduate Schools in the United States takes exception to these projections and in fact anticipates a decline in Ph.D. production in the mid-1970s.[28] Moreover, questions are raised concerning the substantive need for doctoral-trained personnel in the decades ahead as related to the problems facing the society. In effect the Council of Graduate Schools is suggesting that its membership and related types of agencies ought to take responsible leadership in directing the society to provide appropriate levels of high-talent manpower in accordance with the needs of society as seen by these organizations.

In this morass of data and projection there seem to be only two points of agreement. First, that more systematic and sus-

table 8.1

projections of numbers of doctor's degrees (in thousands); some projects are for calendar years and some are for academic years; the distinction is not significant for this paper.

				source of projection and reference				
	Haggstrom (3)			U.S. Office of Education (4)	Hall, National Research Council (2)	National Science Foundation (5)	Cartter (9)	Commission on Human Resources (10)
year	A	B	C					
1971	32.7	32.0	31.9	31.3	30.9	31.4	30.7	29.1
1972	35.8	34.5	34.5	33.8	34.0	33.7	31.3	32.1
1973	38.6	36.9	36.9	37.9	37.1	35.9	32.3	35.5
1974	42.2	39.5	39.2	44.0	40.4	38.4	34.4	39.2
1975	46.6	42.5	41.5	46.6	44.1	39.1	36.0	43.0
1976	52.0	46.0	44.1	50.0	48.5	40.4	38.3	
1977	58.3	49.9	46.7	53.0	53.3	41.4	40.5	
1978	64.8	53.8	49.3	56.6	58.7	42.6	43.5	
1979	71.2	57.8	52.1	59.8	63.4	43.9	45.9	
1980	77.7	61.8	55.0	62.5	68.4	45.2	48.0	
1981	84.0	65.6	57.8				49.8	
1982	90.1	69.1	60.5				51.6	
1983	95.8	72.3	62.9				53.4	
1984	101.0	75.1	64.9				55.2	
1985	105.9	77.6	66.7				56.7	
1990	120.8	87.4	74.1					
1995	116.9	84.1	70.7					
2000	119.7	85.8	72.1					
1971-75	195.9	185.4	184.0	193.6	186.5	178.5	164.7	178.9
1976-80	324.0	269.3	247.2	281.9	292.3	213.5	216.2	
1981-85	476.8	359.7	312.8				266.7	

Source: Dale Wolfle and Charles V. Kidd, "The Future Market for Ph.D.'s," *American Association of University Professors Bulletin*, 58 (March, 1972), 6.

tained effort is needed in identifying and projecting training needs of idea people. Secondly, in the decades ahead an increasing proportion of idea people at the Ph.D. level must anticipate work outside of universities and probably beyond primary research roles.

While considerable doubt is associated with the gross count and projections for idea people, the plurality of universities train within a range of specialty areas. And while there is and can be much mobility of idea people between and among specific career types, most do not shift as far as from biological sciences to engineering sciences, or from the social sciences to the physical sciences, and so on. This is to say for coordination of training to be effective, systematic projections must be generated for major occupational categories and subcategories.

Finally one of the most important aspects of coordinated training for idea manpower is continual retraining in and for new areas of development. It is probable that most of this retraining can most effectively be accomplished by having university educators hold selected training sessions in the agencies and industries that are the employers of idea people. Also such front-line training may well be strengthened by having some regularly employed idea people from agencies serve as part-time instructors on university campuses.

In summary for America to maintain an adequate supply of creative manpower for its needs and a sufficient number of jobs of a stimulating and satisfying type for a post-industrial and cybernating future, systematic manpower policy planning and training are essential.

chapter 1

1. Don K. Price, *The Scientific Estate* (Cambridge: The Belknap Press of Harvard University Press, 1965), pp. 28, 29, 271, 278.

2. Ibid., p. 172.

3. Loc. cit.

4. Ibid., p. 191.

5. Harold L. Wilensky, *Organizational Intelligence* (New York: Basic Books, 1967).

6. Ibid., p. 29.

7. Ibid., p. 11.

8. Loc. cit.

9. Editors of Fortune, *The Mighty Force of Research* (New York: McGraw-Hill, 1956).

10. Ibid., p. vi.

11. Price, op. cit., p. 16.

12. Ibid., p. 57.

13. Ibid., pp. 110, 163.

14. Ibid., p. 277.

15. Ibid., p. vii.

16. James B. Conant, *Modern Science and Modern Man* (New York: Columbia University Press, 1952), pp. 8 *ff.*

17. Ibid., p. 15.

18. Ibid., p. 9.

19. Sanford A. Lakoff, ed., *Knowledge and Power: Essays on Science and Government* (New York: Free Press, 1966), p. 315.

20. Ibid., p. 319.

21. *An Inventory of Congressional Concern with Research and Development* (Washington, D.C.: Sub-Committee on Government Research of the Committee on Government Operations, United States Senate, 1968).

22. Price, op. cit., p. 270.

23. Nicholas J. Demerath, Richard Stephans, and Robb Taylor, *Power, Presidents and Professors* (New York: Basic Books, 1967), p. 19.

24. Heinz Eulau, Harold Quinley, and David D. Henry, *State Officials and Higher Education* (New York: McGraw-Hill, 1970).

25. Ibid., p. 67.

26. Ibid., p. 47.

27. Ibid., p. 167.

28. Eulau, Quinley, and Henry, op. cit., p. 1.

29. Ibid., p. 18.

30. Stanley C. Vance, "Higher Education for the Executive Elite," *California Management Review*, 8 (summer 1966), pp. 21-30.

notes

chapter 2

1. U.S. Census of Population *U.S. Summary* Part D. (Washington, D.C.: U.S. Bureau of the Census), Table 202, and *Tomorrow's Manpower Needs* (Washington, D.C.: U.S. Department of Labor Bulletin 1737, 1972), p. 18.

2. Seymour M. Lipset, "American Intellectuals: Their Politics and Status," *Daedalus* 11 (summer 1959), pp. 460-486.

3. Ibid., p. 460.

4. Ibid., p. 461.

5. Ibid., p. 461; and Anne Roe, *The Making of a Scientist* (New York: Dodd, Mead, 1953), p. 61.

6. Lipset, op. cit., p. 462.

7. Ibid., p. 462.

8. Ibid., p. 463.

9. Ibid., p. 465.

10. Theodore H. White, "The Action Intellectuals," *Life* (June 9, 1967), p. 57.

11. Jay W. Forrester, *Urban Dynamics* (Cambridge, Mass.: MIT Press, 1969); Arnold M. Rose, *The Power Structure* (New York: Oxford University Press, 1967).

12. White, op. cit., p. 57.

13. Ibid., p. 58.

14. Ibid., p. 64.

15. Ibid., p. 65.

16. Ibid., p. 66.

17. Ibid., p. 70.

18. Jacquelyn A. Mattfeld and Carol G. Van Aken, eds., *Women in the Scientific Professions* (Cambridge, Mass.: MIT Press, 1965).

19. Judson Gooding, "The Engineers are Redesigning Their Own Profession: Reeling from the Consequences of Recession and Shifting National Priorities, They are Reexamining their Role in U.S. Society," *Fortune*, 83 (June 1971), pp. 72 ff.

20. Ibid., p. 144.

21. Judson Gooding, "A Fourteen-Week Pressure Cooker for Tomorrow's Top Managers," *Fortune* 85 (February 1972), pp. 109 ff.

22. Loc. cit.

23. Herbert Hoover, "An Engineer Looks at His Profession," in *Engineering: Its Role and Function in Human Society*, ed. by William Henry Davenport, and Daniel Rosenthal (New York: Pergamon Press, 1967), pp. 77-79.

24. *Tomorrow's Manpower Needs*, op. cit.

25. Judson Gooding, "The Engineers are Redesigning their Own Profession," p. 74.

26. *Tomorrow's Manpower Needs*, op. cit.

27. Peter Vanderwicken, "The Angry Young Lawyers," *Fortune* 84 (September 1971), pp. 74 ff.

28. Ibid., p. 74.

29. Ibid., p. 75.

30. Ibid., p. 125.

31. Ibid., p. 125.

32. Ibid., chart 3, p. 9.

33. *Manpower Report of the President* (Washington, D.C.: U.S. Department of Labor, 1970), p. 163.

34. "Comparisons of Earned Degrees Awarded 1901-62 with Projections to 2000," National Science Foundation Publication NSF 6 4-2 (January 13, 1964), p. 13.

35. *U.S. Census of Population 1960 Part D. Table 202.* (Washington, D.C.: Government Printing Office, 1962); and *Tomorrow's Manpower Needs*, op. cit.

36. Loc. cit.

37. *Reviews of Data on Science Resources—National Science Foundation* publication no. 11 (Washington, D.C. NSF December 1966).

38. Edith Wall Andrews and Maurice Moylan, "Scientific and Professional Employment by State Governments," *Monthly Labor*

Review 92 (August 1969), pp. 40-45.

39. "Science and Engineering Professional Manpower Resources in Colleges and Universities," 1961, *Reviews of Data on Research and Development* (National Science Foundation, Washington, D.C. no. 37, January 1963).

40. Floyd Hunter, *Top Leadership, U.S.A.* (Chapel Hill: University of North Carolina Press, 1959).

41. Richard H. Bolt, "The Present Situation of Women Scientists and Engineers in Industry and Government," in *Women in the Scientific Professions,* ed. by Jacquelyn A. Mattfeld and Carol G. Van Aken, (Cambridge, Mass.: 1956), p. 139.

42. Ibid., p. 143.

43. Seymour M. Lipset, "American Intellectuals: Their Politics and Status," *Daedalus* 88 (summer 1959), pp. 460-466.

44. Caryl T. Haskins, "The Changing Environments of Science," *Daedalus* 17 (summer 1965), p. 683.

45. D. C. Pelz and F. M. Andrews, *Scientists in Organizations* (New York: John Wiley, 1967), p. 1.

46. Oscar Handlin, "Science and Technology in Popular Culture," *Daedalus* 94 (winter 1965), pp. 156-170.

47. James B. Conant, *Modern Science and Modern Man* (New York: Columbia University Press, 1952).

48. Ibid., p. 8.

49. Ibid., pp. 8-9.

50. Theodore H. White, "Action-Intellectuals, Scholarly Impact on the Nation's Past," *Life* 62 (June 9, 1967), pp. 56 *ff.*

chapter 3

1. Francis Bello, "The Young Scientists," *Fortune* 49 (June 1954), pp. 142 *ff.*; U.S. Bureau of Labor Statistics, *Occupational Mobility of Scientists* (Washington, D.C.: U.S. Department of Labor Bulletin 1121, February 1953), pp. 1-5; D. C. Pelz and F. M. Andrews, *Scientists in Organizations* (New York: John Wiley 1967).

2. C. Wright Mills, *The Power Elite* (New York: Oxford University Press, 1956), p. 118.

3. Ibid., p. 129.

4. Ibid., p. 158.

5. Ibid., p. 130.

6. A. A. Imberman, "Labor Leaders and Society," *Harvard Business Review* 28 (January 1950), pp. 52-60.

7. Anne Roe, "A Psychological Study of Physical Scientists," *Genetic Psychology Monographs* 43 (May 1951), pp. 229-235; idem, *The Making of A Scientist* (New York: Dodd, Mead, 1953).

8. Anne Roe, *The Making of a Scientist,* op. cit. p. 57.

9. Ibid., p. 88.

10. Ibid., p. 164.

11. Ibid., p. 229.

12. Ibid., p. 232.

13. Paul F. Lazarsfeld and Wagner Thielens, Jr., *The Academic Mind* (Glencoe: Fress Press, 1958).

14. Donald R. Matthews, *U.S. Senators and Their World* (Chapel Hill: University of North Carolina Press, 1960), p. 20.

15. Ibid., p. 44.

16. Pelz and Andrews, op. cit.

17. Harvey C. Lehman, *Age and Achievement* (Princeton: Princeton University Press, 1953), pp. 324-327.

18. Loc. cit.

19. Ibid., pp. 328-329.

20. Anne Roe, *The Making of a Scientist,* op. cit., p. 61.

21. Anne Roe, "A Psychological Study of Physical Scientists," op. cit., p. 231.

22. Anne Roe, *The Making of a Scientist,* op. cit. p. 60.

23. Charles G. McClintock, Charles B. Spaulding and Henry A. Turner, "Political Orientation of Academically Affiliated Psychologists," *American Psychologist* 20 (February 1965), pp. 211-221; "Political Orientation of Academically Affiliated Sociologists," *Sociology and Social Research* 47 (April 1963), pp. 273-289; and H. A. Turner, et al., "The Political Party Affiliation of American Political Scientists," *Western Political Quarterly* 16 (September 1963), pp. 650-665.

chapter 4

1. *Formal Occupational Training of Adult Workers* (Washington, D.C.: Manpower/Automation Research, Monograph No. 2, 1964); Lee Taylor, *Occupational Sociology* (New York: Oxford University Press, 1968), p. 229.

2. Neil W. Chamberlain, "Re-Tooling the Mind," *Atlantic Monthly* (September 1964), pp. 48-50. See also Taylor, op. cit.

3. Chamberlain, op. cit., p. 48.

4. Audrey F. Borenstein, "The Ethical Ideal of the Professions: A Sociological Analysis of the Academic and Medical Professions," (Ph.D. Thesis, Louisiana State University, Baton Rouge, 1958).

5. Chamberlain, op. cit., p. 50.

6. Loc. cit.

7. *College Educated Workers, 1968-80: A Study of Supply and Demand* (Washington, D.C.: U.S. Department of Labor, Bulletin 1676, 1970); see also *Jobs for the 1970's Slide Series* (Washington, D.C.: U.S. Department of Labor, 1972).

8. Laurence B. DeWitt and A. Dale Tussing, *The Supply and Demand for Graduates of Higher Education: 1970 to 1980* (Syracuse: EPPC Publications, 1206 Harrison Street, New York, 13210, 1972).

9. "Ph.D. Surplus Seen Over Estimated," *The Chronicle of Higher Education* 21 (March 20, 1972), p. 3, and *Higher Education and National Affairs* (March 10, 1972), p. 11.

10. Ibid, p. 1.

11. Ibid, p. 2.

12. Kenneth A. Simon and Martin M. Grankel, *Projections of Educational Statistics to 1980-81* (Washington, D.C.: U.S. Department of Health, Education and Welfare Publication No. (OE) 72-99, 1972) p. 26.

13. Loc. cit.

14. John D. Millet, *The Academic Community,* (New York: McGraw-Hill, 1962).

15. Philip W. Semas, "Bachelor's Degree in Three Years Gaining Favor," *The Chronicle of Higher Education* 6 (January 1972), p. 1, 5.

16. John D. Millett, *Decision Making and Administration in Higher Education* (Kent, Ohio: Kent State University Press, 1968), pp. 115 ff.

17. *Graduate Education—Parameters for Policy* (Washington, D.C.: National Science Board, 1969).

18. *The Chronicle of Higher Education* 6 (April 17, 1972), p. 1.

19. A. J. Braumbaugh, *Establishing New Senior Colleges* (Atlanta: Southern Regional Education Board, 1966).

20. Ibid., p. 53.

21. Ibid., pp. 72, 75.

22. Ibid., p. 77.

23. Alexander W. Astin, "Undergraduate Institutions and the Production of Scientists," *Science* 141 (July 26, 1963), pp. 334-338.

24. Loc. cit.

25. James A. Davis, *Great Aspirations: The Graduate School Plans of America's College Seniors* (Chicago: Aldine, 1964), p. 1.

26. K. A. Simon and W. V. Grant, *Digest of Educational Statistics 1971* (Washington, D.C.: U.S. Department of Health, Education and Welfare, Publication No. (OE) 72-45, 1972), p. 67.

27. Davis, op. cit.

28. Ibid., p. 46.

29. Ibid., p. 62.

30. Allan M. Cartter, *An Assessment of Quality in Graduate Education* (Washington, D.C.: American Council on Education, 1966), p. ix.

31. Dael Wolfle and Charles V. Kidd, "The Future Market for Ph.D.'s," *American Association of University Professors Bulletin* 58 (March 1972, pp. 5-16.

32. Martin Frankel, *Projections of Educational Statistics to 1980-81* (Washington, D.C.: U.S. Office of Education, 1971), p. 45.

33. *Graduate Education—Parameters for Policy*, op. cit., p. 3; Walter Crosby Eells, *Degrees In Higher Education* (Washington, D.C.: The Center for Applied Research in Education Incorporated, 1963); Bernard Berelson, *Graduate Education in the United States* (New York: McGraw-Hill, 1961); Everett Walters, "The Rise of Graduate Education," in *Graduate Education Today* ed. by Everett Walters (Washington, D.C.: American Council of Education, 1965).

34. Cartter, op. cit., p. 118.

35. A. M. Cartter and R. Farrell, "Higher Education in Last Third of the Century," *Educational Record*, (spring 1965), pp. 119-128.

36. Cartter, op. cit., p. 119.

37. Ibid., p. 119.

38. Ibid., p. 119.

39. Wolfle and Kidd, op. cit., p. 8.

40. Ibid., p. 9.

41. Ibid., p. 40.

42. George L. Gropper and Robert Fitzpatrick, *Who Goes to Graduate School?* (Pittsburgh: American Institute for Research, 1959); Ann M. Heiss, *Challenges to Graduate Schools* (San Francisco: Jossey-Bass, 1970), see especially Chapter 6; Charles M. Grigg, *Recruitment to Graduate Study* (Atlanta: Southern Regional Education Board, 1965); *Two Years After the College Degree* (Washington, D.C.: National Science Foundation, 1963); James A. Davis, *Great Aspirations* (Chicago: Aldine, 1964); Norman Miller, *One Year after Commencement* (Chicago: National Opinion Research Center, 1963).

43. Grigg, op. cit., p. 50.

44. Heiss, op. cit., pp. 92 *ff.*

45. Ibid., p. 94.

46. Ibid., p. 102.

47. John A. Creager, *The American Graduate Student: A Normative Description* (Washington, D.C.: American Council of Education, 1971); see also Ann M. Heiss, op. cit., Chapter 10, "Student Appraisals of Ph.D. Programs."

48. John L. Snell, "The Master's Degree," in *Graduate Education Today*, ed. by Everett Walters, (Washington, D.C.: American Council of Education, 1965), and *The Chronicle of Higher Education* 6 (April 17, 1972), p. 1.

49. Walter E. Tolliver, *Earned Degrees 1961-62* (Washington, D.C.: Government Printing Office (OE-54013-62), 1963), p. 7.

50. Oliver, op. cit., pp. 16-36.

51. Snell, op. cit., p. 82.

52. *The Chronicle of Higher Education*, op. cit.

53. Oliver C. Carmichael, *Graduate Education: A Critique and a Program* (New York: Harper, 1961), Chapter 11; see also Berelson, op. cit., pp. 185 *ff.*; and Charles M. Grigg, *Graduate Education* (New York: The Center for Applied Research in Education, 1965), pp. 55 *ff.*

54. Unpublished Tables from the National Center for Educational Statistics as reported in *The Chronicle of Higher Education,* 6 (April 17, 1972), p. 1.

55. Nicholas J. Demerath and others, *Power, Presidents, and Professors* (New York: Basic Books, 1967); and *Selected Financial Statistics of Institutions of Higher Education 1968-69* (Washington, D.C.: National Center for Educational Statistics, 1969); see also Philip H. Coombs, "The University and Its External Environment," in *The Changing University,* ed. by George J. Daigneault (Chicago: Center for the Study of Liberal Education for Adults, 1959).

56. Demerath, op. cit., p. 6.

57. Paul F. Mertins and Norman J. Brandt, *Financial Statistics of Institutions of Higher Education: Current Funds Revenue and Expenditures 1968-69* (Washington, D.C.: National Center for Educational Statistics, 1969).

58. Frankel, op. cit., p. 45.

59. *Educational Directory 1971-72, Higher Education* (Washington, D.C.: National Center for Educational Statistics, 1972).

60. Paul F. Mertins, *Financial Statistics of Institutions of Higher Education: Federal Funds 1965-66 and 1966-67* (Washington, D.C.: National Center for Educational Statistics, 1967).

61. Paul F. Mertins, *Financial Statistics of Institutions of Higher Education: Property 1966-67* (Washington, D.C.: National Center for Educational Statistics, 1967).

chapter 5

1. Stephen R. Graubard, "Preface," *Daedalus* 94 (winter 1965), p. 685.

2. Harold L. Wilensky, *Organizational Intelligence* (New York: Basic Books, 1967), p. viii.

3. Seymour M. Lipset, "American Intellectuals: Their Politics and Status," *Daedalus* 11 (summer 1959), p. 467.

4. Theodore H. White, "The Action Intellectuals," Part I, *Life* (June 9, 1967), p. 49.

5. Ibid., Part III, (June 23, 1967), p. 77.

6. Sanford A. Lakoff, ed., *Knowledge and Power: Essays on Science and Government* (New York: Free Press, 1966), p. 319.

7. Derek J. DeSolla Price, *Science Since Babylon* (New Haven: Yale University Press, 1962).

8. Alexander King, "Research and Political Power," *Science* 126 (August 1957), pp. 237-238.

9. William J. Price and Lawrence W. Bass, "Scientific Research and the Innovative Process," *Science* 164 (May 16, 1969), pp. 802-806.

10. Ibid., p. 805.

11. "R and D Investment Leveling Off: NSF," *Chronicle of Higher Education* (August 23, 1967), p. 16.

12. "Research Funds Used in the Nation's Scientific Endeavor," *Reviews of Data on Scientific Resources, NSF,* vol. 1, (May 1965), p. 1.

13. *College and University Reports, December 24, 1971,* (Washington, D.C.: Commerce Clearing House, 1971), p. 3.

14. White, op. cit., Part I.

15. Jay W. Forrester, *World Dynamics* (Cambridge, Mass.: Wright-Allen Press, 1971); idem, *Urban Dynamics* (Cambridge, Mass.: MIT Press, 1969); idem., *Industrial Dynamics* (Cambridge, Mass.: MIT Press, 1961).

16. B. F. Skinner, *Beyond Freedom and Dignity* (New York: Bantam Books, 1971).

17. William R. Burch, Jr., *Daydreams and Nightmares* (New York: Harper, 1971).

18. Marilyn E. Ludwig, "Architectural Research Comes of Age," *American Institute of Architects Journal* 44 (November 1965), p. 6.

19. Ben H. Evans, "Architecture and Research," *American Institute of Architects Journal* 45 (June 1966).

20. Dael Wolfle, "Government Organization of Science," *Science* 131 (May 13, 1960), pp. 1407-1417; Charles E. Falk, *Science and Technical Personnel in the Federal Government* (Washington, D.C.: National Science Foundation, 1964).

21. George B. Kistiakowsky, "On Federal Support of Basic Research" *Daedalus* 94 (summer 1965), p. 728.

22. Wolfle, op. cit.; and A. H. Dupree, *Science in the Federal Government* (Cambridge, Mass.: Belknap Press of Harvard University Press, 1957).

23. Wolfle, op. cit.

24. Irving Louis Horowitz, "The Life and Death of Project Camelot," *Trans-Action* 3 (November-December 1965), p. 3 ff.

25. Jay Jacobs, "What the Federal Arts Program Really Means," *Art in America* 55 (March-April), pp. 25-59.

26. "Funds for Performance of Research and Development in American Industry, 1960," *Reviews of Data on Research and Development, NSF, NO.* 30 (September 1961).

27. Loc. cit.

28. "Research and Development in American Industry, 1963," *Reviews of Data on Science Resources, NSF,* vol. 1 (December 1964).

29. "The Corporation as a Creative Environment," *Kaiser News* 1 (1972); Walter Guzzardi, Jr., *The Young Executives* (New York: New American Library, 1964); Anthony Jay, *The Corporation Man* (New York: Random House, 1971); and Charles Reich, *The Greening of America* (New York: Random House, 1970).

30. *Kaiser News*, op. cit.

31. Ibid., pp. 26-27.

32. "Bright Young Men Choose Business Careers," *Nation's Business* 54 (June 1966), pp. 46 ff.

33. David Bendel Hertz, "The Creative Mentality in Industrial Research," in *Human Relations in Industrial Research Management*, ed. by Robert T. Livingston and Stanley H. Milberg (New York: Columbia University Press, 1957),p. 45.

34. Dan Cordtz, "There is Another Generation of Whiz Kids at Ford," *Fortune* 75 (January 1967), p. 183.

35. Francis Bello, "The Young Scientist," *Fortune* 49 (June 1954), 176; and Harold Gershinowitz, "Industrial Research Programs and Academic Research," *American Scientist* 46 (March 1958), pp. 24-32.

36. Gershinowitz, op. cit., pp. 27-28.

37. Ibid., p. 28.

38. Maurice Nelles, *Functions of Research and Engineering* (New York: American Management As-

sociation, Research and Development Series No. 3, 1957), pp. 12-20.

39. James B. Conant, *Modern Science and Modern Man* (New York: Columbia University Press, 1952).

40. White, op. cit., Part I, p. 47.

41. Ibid., pp. 43, 68.

42. Ibid., p. 72.

43. Daniel P. Moynihan, *The Negro Family: The Case for National Action* (Washington, D.C.: U.S. Department of Labor, Office of Policy, Planning and Research, March 1965).

44. Lee Rainwater and William L. Yancey, *The Moynihan Report and the Politics of Controversy* (Cambridge, Mass.: MIT Press, 1967).

45. Ibid., p. 19.

46. Ibid., pp. 300, 302, 307.

47. Edward H. Hobbs, *Behind the President* (Washington, D.C.: Public Affairs Press, 1954).

48. Wilensky, op. cit.; Corinne Silverman, *The President's Economic Advisors,* (Tuskaloosa: University of Albama Press, 1959); and Edwin G. Norse and Bertram M. Gross, "The Role of the Council of Economic Advisors," *The American Political Science Review* 42 (April 1948).

49. "Faculty Consulting: College and University Policies, Practices, and Problems," *Reviews of Data on Science Resources, NSF,* No. 8 (February 1966).

50. Daniel Paitich, "The Clinical Psychologist as Expert Witness: A Dialogue," *Canadian Psychologist* 7 (October 1966), pp. 407-412.

51. "Federal Liaison/Architects Named to GSA Design Panel," *American Institute of Architects Journal* 44 (Nov. 1965), p. 10, 18

52. "Professional Collaboration in Environmental Design," *American Institute of Architects Journal* 46 (July 1966), pp. 66-68

53. Bryce Nelson, "Scientists Plan Research Strike at M.I.T. on 4 March," *Science* 163 (January 24, 1969), p. 373.

54. Loc. cit.; and Bryce Nelson, "M.I.T.'s March 4: Scientists Discuss Renouncing Military Research," *Science* 163 (March 14, 1969).

55. Dore Ashton, "The Artist as Dissenter," Studio 171 (April 1966), pp. 164 ff.; idem; "Los Angeles: Tower for Peace," *Art News* 65 (April 1966, pp. 25, 71.

56. Loc. cit.

57. Erwin A. Glikes and Paul Schwaber, eds., *Of Poetry and Power* (New York: Basic Books, 1964).

58. White, op. cit., Part I, p. 44.

59. Conant, op. cit., p. 59.

60. R. L. Sproull, "Federal Support of Science and Technology," in *Science and Society: A Symposium* (New York, Benjamin, 1965).

61. "Nixon Budget Contains Increases for Number of Higher Education Programs," *Higher Education and National Affairs* 21 (January 28, 1972).

62. Richard E. Neustadt, *Presidential Power* (New York: John Wiley, 1960).

63. Emmet John Hughes, *The Ordeal of Power* (New York: Atheneum, 1963), p. 133.

64. Richard F. Fenno, Jr., *The President's Cabinet* (Cambridge, Mass.: Harvard University Press, 1959).

65. Ibid., p. 119.

66. Bertram D. Thomas, "Our New Civilization: An Age of Research," in *Science and Society: A Symposium* (New York, Benjamin, 1965), p. 29.

67. Irving Louis Horowitz, ed., *Power, Politics and People: The Collected Essays of C. Wright Mills* (New York: Oxford University Press, 1963).

68. David P. Gardner, *The California Oath Controversy* (Berkeley: University of California Press, 1967).

69. Ibid., p. 27.

70. Ibid., p. 55.

chapter 6

1. William H. Whyte, Jr., *The Organization Man* (New York: Doubleday Anchor, 1956); and Alvan W. Gouldner, "Cosmopolitans and Locals: Toward an Analysis of Latent Social Roles," *Administrative Science Quarterly* 2 (December 1957), pp. 281-306.

2. J. C. Raaen, "Effective Utilization of Scientific Manpower," in *Engineering and Research in Small and Medium-Size Companies* (New York: American Management Association, Research and Development Series No. 3, 1957), pp. 66-72.

3. Angus Campbell, "Administering Research Organizations," *American Psychologist* 8 (June 1953), pp. 225-230.

4. Ibid., pp. 226-227.

5. Loc. cit.

6. Daniel S. Greenberg, "Congress Looks at Science," *American Psychologist* 19 (February 1964), pp. 102-104.

7. Spencer Klaw, *The New Brahmins: Scientific Life in America* (New York: William Morrow, 1968).

8. "Government Labs: Britain's Harwell Finds New Role in Industrial Work," *Science* 163 (March 7, 1969), pp. 1041-1044.

9. D. C. Pelz and F. M. Andrews, *Scientists in Organizations* (New York: John Wiley, 1967); and Lee Taylor, *Occupational Sociology* (New York: Oxford University Press, 1968), ch. 22.

10. Anne Roe, "The Psychology of the Scientist," *Scientific Manpower 1960* (Washington, D.C.: National Science Foundation, Government Printing Office, 1961), pp. 48-52.

11. Ibid., p. 49.

12. Ibid., pp. 51-52.

13. Barry Ulanov, *The Two Worlds of American Art* (New York: Macmillan, 1965), p. 16.

14. Gouldner, op. cit.; Peter M. Blau and W. Richard Scott, *Formal Organization* (San Francisco: Chandler, 1962); Taylor, op. cit.; and Lowell W. Steele, "Personal Practices in Industrial Laboratories," in *Human Relations in Industrial Research and Management*, ed. by Robert T. Livingston and Stanley H. Milbert (New York: Columbia University Press, 1957).

15. Pelz and Andrews, op. cit., p. 212.

16. David Riesman, "The Academic Career: Notes on Recruitment and Colleagueship," *Daedalus* 88 (winter 1959), pp. 147-169.

17. Stephen R. Graubard and Gerald Holton, *Excellence and Leadership in a Democracy* (New York: Columbia University Press, 1962).

18. William Attwood, "The Labyrinth in Foggy Bottom: A Critique of the State Department," *The Atlantic Monthly* 219 (February 1967), pp. 45-50.

19. Logan Wilson, *The Academic Man* (New York: Octagon Books, 1964).

20. Taylor, op. cit., see especially chapter 17 on colleagueship.

21. Seymour M. Lipset, "American Intellectuals: Their Politics and Status," *Daedalus* 11 (summer 1959), p. 478.

22. Whyte, op. cit., pp. 242-243.

23. Riesman, op. cit., p. 155.

24. Ibid., p. 156.

25. Taylor, op. cit., chapter 17.

26. Edmund L. Van Deusen, "The Inventor in Eclipse," in Editors of Fortune, *The Mighty Force of Research* (New York: McGraw-Hill, 1956), p. 77 *ff*.

27. Francis Bello, "The Young Scientist," *Fortune* 49 (June, 1954), p. 182.

28. Loc. cit.

29. Lawrence S. Kubie, "Some Unsolved Problems of the Scientific Career, Part I," *American Scientist* 41 (October 1953), p. 596.

30. Whyte, op. cit., p. 166.

31. Kubie, Part II, op. cit., p. 108.

32. Kubie, Part I, op. cit., p. 597.

33. Ibid., p. 598.

34. Ibid., p. 605.

35. Ibid., p. 610.

36. "Secrecy and Dissemination in Science and Technology," *Science* 163 (February 21, 1969), pp. 787-790.

37. Oscar M. Ruebhausen and Orville G. Brim, Jr., "Privacy and Behavioral Research," *American Psychologist* 21 (May 1966), pp. 423-437.

38. *Privacy and Behavioral Research* (Washington, D.C.: Office of Science and Technology, Government Printing Office, 1967).

39. Ibid., p. 5.

40. Irving L. Horowitz, "The Life and Death of Project Camelot," *Trans-Action* 3 (November-December 1965), pp. 3 *ff*.

41. "Salaries and Selected Characteristics of U.S. Scientists, 1968," *NSF Reviews of Data on Science Resources*, No. 16 (December 1968).

42. Campbell, op. cit.

43. Loc. cit.

44. *American Science Manpower: 1970* (Washington, D.C.: National Science Foundation, 1972), p. 7.

45. C. Wright Mills, *The Power Elite* (New York: Oxford University Press, 1956), p. 156.

46. Steele, op. cit., p. 350.

47. Harold Seymour, "Call Me Doctor," *The Educational Record* 39 (July 1958), pp. 230-234.

48. Kubie, Part II, op. cit., p. 111.

49. Loc. cit.

50. Pelz and Andrews, op. cit., p. 139.

51. Roger M. Blough, "Business Can Satisfy the Young Intellectual," *Harvard Business Review* 44 (January-February 1966), p. 53.

52. Pelz and Andrews, op. cit., p. 3.

chapter 7

1. Roger M. Blough, "Business Can Satisfy the Young Intellectual," *Harvard Business Review* 44 (January-February 1966), pp. 49-57; and C. Wright Mills, *The Power Elite* (New York: Oxford University Press, 1956), pp. 118 *ff*.

2. Lewis A. Coser, *Men of Ideas* (New York: Free Press, 1965), p. 305.

3. As quoted in J. Stefan Dupré and S. A. Lakoff, *Science and the Nation* (Englewood Cliffs, N. J.: Prentice-Hall, 1962).

4. Coser, op. cit., p. 309.

5. "Research and Development and the Gross National Product," *NSF Reviews of Data on Research and Development*, No. 26 (February 1961).

6. Seymour M. Lipset, "American Intellectuals: Their Politics and Status," *Daedalus* 11 (summer 1951), pp. 473 *ff.*

7. "Lincoln Center: A New Pattern in Culture," *The American Way* 1 (November 4, 1968).

8. Walter G. Berl, "AAAS Meetings: A Progress Report," *Science* 163 (February 21, 1969).

9. Richard Swalin, "Athelstan Spilhaus, President-Elect," *Science* 163 (February 21, 1969), pp. 831-832.

10. • Paul S. Greenlaw, et al., *Business Simulation in Industrial and University Education* (Englewood, Cliffs, N. J.: Prentice-Hall, 1962); and Lowell W. Herron, *Executive Action Simulation* (Englewood Cliffs, N. J.: Prentice-Hall, 1960).

11. "The California Tomorrow Plan: A First Sketch," *Ekistics* 32 (August 1971), pp. 106-113.

12. Stewart Alsop and Thomas Braden, *Sub-Rosa* (New York: Cornwall Press, 1946).

13. Allen Dulles, *The Craft of Intelligence* (New York: Harper, 1963).

14. Charles E. Wyzanski, Jr., "The Lawyer's Relation to Recent Social Legislation," in *Whereas — A Judge's Premises* (Boston: Little, Brown, 1965), pp. 206 *ff.*

15. Coser, op. cit., p. 310.

16. "Anti-War Protests Follow U.S. Bombings of North Vietnam," *Higher Education and National Affairs* 21 (April 21, 1972), p. 2.

17. "The Artist as Social Critic," *Print* 20 (January 1966), pp. 32-37.

18. Rima Drell Reck, *Literature and Responsibility* (Baton Rouge: Louisiana State University Press, 1969).

19. Allen Ginsberg, *Howl and Other Poems* (San Francisco: City Lights Books, 1959), pp. 21-22; and LeRoi Jones, *The Dead Lecturer* (New York: Grove Press, 1964),

20. Donald B. Day, compiler, *Index to Science-Fiction Magazines, 1926-1950* (Portland, Oregon: Perri Press, 1952).

21. "Biological Warfare: Is the Smithsonian Really a 'Cover'?" *Science* 163 (February 21, 1969), pp. 791 *ff.*

22. E. M. McCormick, "Digital Computers: Their History, Operation, and Use," in *Smithsonian Treasury of 20th Century Science,* ed. Webster P. True, (New York: Simon and Schuster, 1966) pp. 171 *ff.*

23. "National Data Bank: Its Advocates Try to Erase 'Big Brother' Image," *Science* 163 (January 10, 1969), pp. 160 *ff.*

24. James Martin and Adrian R. D. Norman, *The Computerized Society* (Englewood Cliffs, N. J.: Prentice-Hall, 1970).

25. Donald N. Michael, *Cybernation: The Silent Conquest* (Santa Barbara, California: Center for the Study of Democratic Institutions, 1962); and Donald M. McKay, "What is Cybernetics?" op. cit., pp. 417 *ff.*

26. Herbert Krosney, *Beyond Welfare* (New York: Holt, 1966).

27. John Maynard Smith, "Eugenics and Utopia," *Daedalus* 94 (spring 1965), pp. 487 *ff.*

28. Leo Davids, "North American Marriage: 1990," *The Futurist* (October 1971), pp. 190-194.

29. Roy O. Greep, *Human Fertility and Population·Problems* (Cambridge: Schenkman, 1963).

30. Fred Warshofsky, *The Control of Life* (New York: Viking, 1969).

31. Loc. cit.

32. David D. Rustein, *The Coming Revolution in Medicine* (Cambridge, Mass.: MIT Press, 1967); and James S. Coleman, et al., *Medical Innovation* (New York: Bobbs-Merrill, 1966).

33. Editors of Fortune, *The Mighty Force of Research* (New York: McGraw-Hill, 1956), p. 37.

34. Roy Danish, "The Longest Journey—A Symposium," *Television Quarterly* 5 (spring 1966), pp. 41 ff.

35. Leo Bogart, *The Age of Television* (New York: Frederick Ungar, 1956).

36. Herbert E. Alexander, "Political Broadcasting," *Television Quarterly* 5 (spring 1966), pp. 65 ff.

37. Danish, op. cit., p. 41.

38. "TV and the Political Institution," *Television Quarterly* 5 (winter 1966), p. 8.

39. E. William Henry, et al., "Section 315: The Prospects," *Television Quarterly* 5 (winter 1966), p. 35.

40. Herbert E. Alexander, et al., "The High Cost of TV Campaigning," *Television Quarterly* 5 (winter 1966), p. 48.

41. Charles S. Steinberg, "The McLuhan Myth," *Television Quarterly* 6 (summer 1967), pp. 7-16.

42. Carl I. Hovland, "Effects of the Mass Media of Communication," in *Mass Media and Communication*, ed. by Charles S. Steinberg (New York: Hasting House, 1966).

43. Leonard Mandelbaum, "Apollo: How the United States Decided to Go to the Moon," *Science* (February 14, 1969), pp. 649-654.

44. *The Mighty Force of Research*, op. cit.

45. Loc. cit.

46. Loc. cit.

47. Loc. cit.

48. Loc. cit.

49. J. Eugene Haas, et al., "Science Technology and the Public: The Case of Planned Weather Modification," in *Social Behavior, Natural Resources, and the Environment*, ed. by William R. Burch, Neil H. Cheek, Jr., and Lee Taylor (New York: Harper, 1972).

50. Lee Taylor and A. R. Jones, Jr., *Rural Life and Urbanized Society* (New York: Oxford University Press, 1964); see especially chapters 11 and 12.

51. Francis Bello, "The Peaceful Atom," in Editors of Fortune, *The Mighty Force of Research* (New York: McGraw-Hill, 1956), pp. 196 ff.

52. Loc. cit.

53. John McHale, "World Facts and Trends: Energy and Materials," *Ekistics* 32 (August 1971), pp. 153-157.

54. C. A. Doxiadis, *Ekistics: An Introduction to the Science of Human Settlements* (New York: Oxford University Press, 1968); see also numerous articles in the journal *Ekistics* from 1960 to 1972, with special emphasis on the August 1971 issue devoted to "Ecumenopolis: City of the Future."

55. John G. Papaioannou, "Future Urbanization Patterns: A Long-Range World-Wide View," *Ekistics* 32 (August 1971), pp. 368-381.

56. Loc. cit.

57. C. A. Doxiadis, "Man's Movement and His Settlements," *Ekistics*, 29 (May 1970), pp. 316-321.

58. Eric Hodgins, "The Strange State of American Research," in *The Mighty Force of Research*, op. cit., p. 7.

59. "Diffusion of Technological

Change," *NSF Reviews of Data on Research and Development*, No. 31 (October 1961).

chapter 8

1. "Technology's New Political Environment: Part I—The Government's Expanding Role," *Innovation* 27 (January 1972), pp. 5-8.

2. Ibid., p. 12.

3. Don K. Price, *The Scientific Estate* (Cambridge, Mass.: The Belknap Press of Harvard University Press, 1965), p. 11.

4. Ibid., pp. 16, 24, 28.

5. Ibid., pp. 72, 76.

6. Ibid., p. 172.

7. Ibid., p. 242.

8. Ibid., p. 257; and Dael Wolfle, "Government Organization of Science," *Science* 131 (May 13, 1960), pp. 1407-1417; and "A Bill to Establish a Department of Science, Research and Technology," H. R. 464, 91st Congress 1st session, House of Representatives.

9. Theodore H. White, "The Action Intellectuals," Part I, *Life* 62 (June 9, 1967).

10. Howard Mumford Jones, "Modern Scholarship and the Data of Greatness," in *Boston College Centennial Colloquiums, 1963—The Knowledge Explosion*, ed. by Francis W. Sweeney (New York: Farrar, Strauss & Giroux, 1966), p. 27.

11. Price, op. cit.

12. Robert Boguslaw, *The New Utopians* (Englewood Cliffs, N. J.: Prentice-Hall, 1965).

13. Carl W. Fischer, "Scientist and Statesman: A Profile of the Organization of the President's Science Advisory Committee," in *Knowledge and Power: Essays on Science and Government*, ed. by

Sanford A. Lakoff (New York: Free Press, 1966), p. 315.

14. Ibid., p. 316.

15. Jerome B. Wiesner, "Federal Research and Development: Policies and Prospects," *American Psychologists* 19 (February 1964), pp. 97-99.

16. "Scientists and Legislation," *Science* 126 (October 1957), p. 635.

17. Clinton P. Anderson, "Scientific Advice for Congress," *Science* 144 (April 3, 1964), pp. 29-30.

18. Derek J. De Solla Price, *Little Science, Big Science* (New York: Columbia University Press, 1963), pp. v-vi.

19. *Tomorrow's Manpower Needs* (Washington, D.C.: U.S. Department of Labor, Bulletin 1737, 1972); and Eli Ginzberg, *Manpower Agenda for America* (New York: McGraw-Hill, 1968).

20. "American Civilization and Its Leadership Needs, 1960-1990," *The Annals of the American Academy of Political and Social Science* 325 (September 1959).

21. Edith Wall Andrews and Maurice Moylan, "Scientific and Professional Employment by State Governments," *Monthly Labor Review* 92 (August 1969), pp. 40-45.

22. Michael F. Crowley, "Ph.D. Holders in Private Industry," *Monthly Labor Review* 93 (August 1970), p. 65.

23. Ralph E. Lapp "Where the Brains Are," *Fortune* 73 (March 1966), pp. 155 ff.

24. Heinz Eulau, *State Officials and Higher Education* (New York: McGraw-Hill, 1970).

25. Dael Wolfle and Charles V. Kidd, "The Future Market for Ph.D.'s," *American Association of University Professors Bulletin* 58 (March 1972), pp. 5-16.

26. David Metz, "Ph.D.'s Should be Planned," *New Scientist* (February 17, 1972), pp. 386-388.

27. Phillip H. Ableson, "Federal Support of Graduate Education," *Science* 175 (March 3, 1972), p. 947.

28. "Graduate Schools Deny Large Ph.D. Production on Way—See Future Dip," *Higher Education and National Affairs* 21 (April 28, 1972), p. 3; and "Ph.D. Surplus Seen Over Estimated," *The Chronicle of Higher Education* (March 20, 1972), p. 3.

index